tsk

tsk

selected works

CONTENTS

UNBUILT

LEGACY

APPENDIX

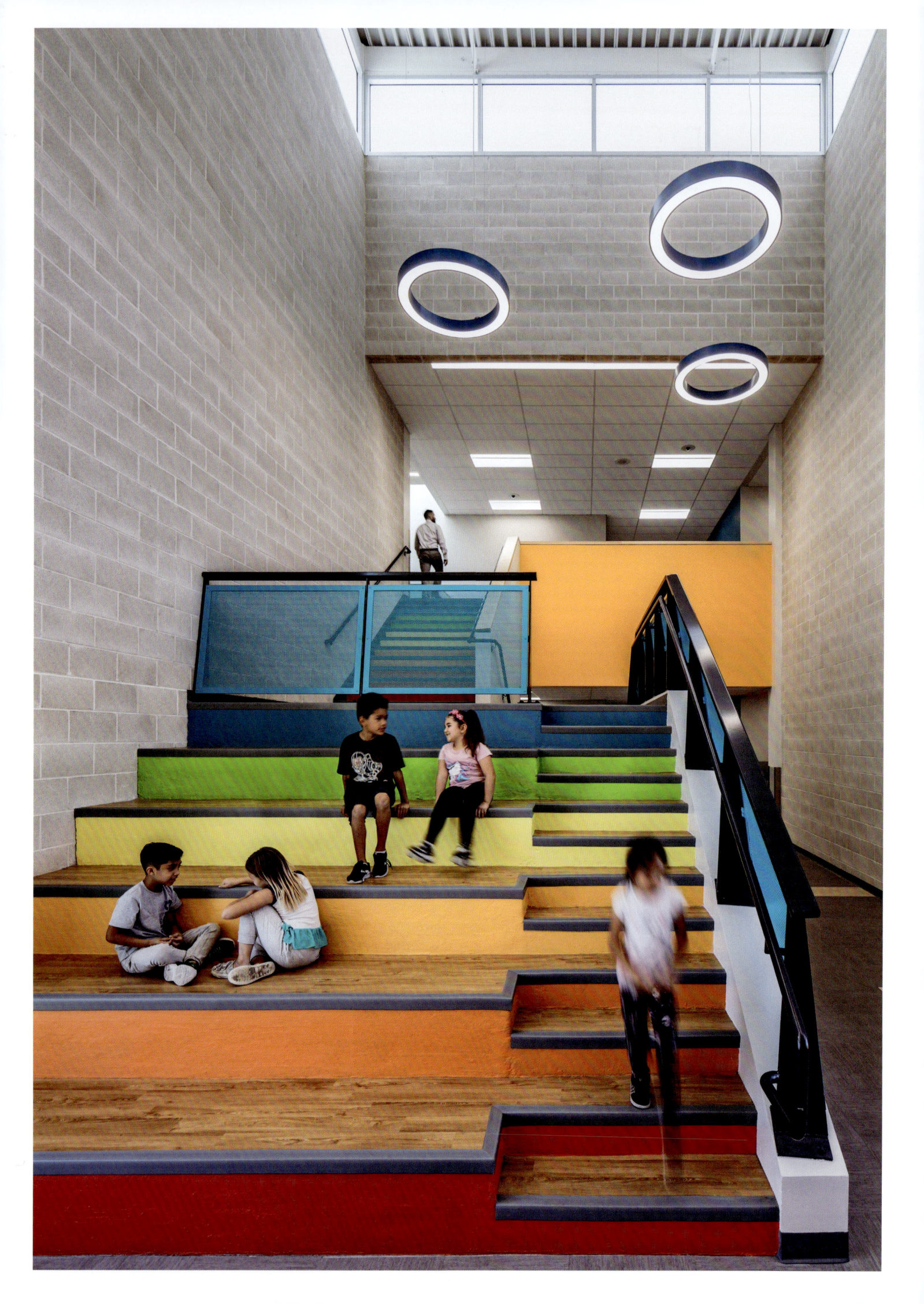

REALLY LEARNING FROM LAS VEGAS: THE WORK OF WINDOM KIMSEY AND TSK

Aaron Betsky

Las Vegas Architects

It is hard to avoid the work of Windom Kimsey and TSK in Las Vegas. If you arrive there as a visitor through Harry Reid International Airport, you will see the control tower the firm designed as you taxi in and there is an even chance you will deplane through the lofty expanse of the D Gates Terminal it authored. If you are coming there for a convention, you cannot avoid the sweep of the canopy that arches over the 1.44-million-square-foot (133,780-square-meter) West Hall addition to the municipal facility. If you happen to be a native, you will know the Clark County Regional Justice Center Kimsey was responsible for designing, as it towers over downtown and is the sight of many a controversial court trial. You might encounter the firm's architecture when you get your driver's license at the DMV Sahara Service Center. You or your kids might be educated at one of the dozens of elementary, middle school, high school, community college, or university buildings they have designed in the area.

TSK is by far the most dominant design firm of what is now, with well over two million inhabitants, the twenty-eighth-largest metropolitan area in the United States—and one of the most visited tourist destinations. Yet there is a good chance you will not have heard of the firm or Kimsey. That is because the one place where you will not encounter TSK's architecture is in buildings for which Las Vegas is known, namely its hotels, casinos, and all the razzle-dazzle retail, entertainment, and shopping that goes with that world. TSK are Las Vegas' native architects, the ones who design the places where people work, live, learn, and play. Not only that, the firm designs many structures that would seem to resist architecture, and that makes its contributions not as noticeable as they should be.

The position it has taken in the field is a difficult one, and one of the reasons TSK and its predecessor firm, Tate & Snyder, has not received very much critical attention is that the space and place for good architecture in that *other*—which is to say, most of—Las Vegas is extremely limited. The Strip and the entertainment industry take up all the attention, exactly because it thrives on such visual and experiential notoriety. What you notice in Las Vegas are the places that use architecture as part of their signage and storytelling. When Robert Venturi, Denise Scott-Brown, and Steve Izenour were *Learning from Las Vegas*, that was what they were seeing. The rest of the metropolis, with its endless acres of suburban developments, office parks, warehouses, and factories, permeated by empty lots in the kind of "holey development" typical of the American Southwest, and surrounded by a rock desert landscape of considerable drama, remained out of their and subsequent critics' purview.

Beyond that conceptual and perceptional issue, the reason why Tate & Snyder's and TSK's architecture is not noticed is that it's often hard to find. Beyond the Strip, Las Vegas and the other municipalities and institutions in the area have little use for architecture. The casinos—but also the air-force bases and other federal facilities, factories, and back-office and trans-shipment businesses—have brought wealth to the Las Vegas area, but not a great deal of public surplus. Living on minimal taxes in a culture devoted to risk with only a base social support or cushion, the budgets of public and governmental institutions are bare-bones. For years, the local school system thought it could not even afford windows in its high schools. Working in that environment, TSK has worked hard to wrest good space, contributions to the context, and a degree of community identity out of the most basic materials and elements of architecture.

TSK is currently led by Windom Kimsey, who joined what was George Tate's firm and rose up to a leadership position when Bill Snyder joined Tate to form Tate & Snyder. In 2008, he took over as the president and CEO and, after Snyder's retirement, rebranded the firm as TSK. Originally from Tennessee, Kimsey was educated at the University of Michigan and then studied there (with one of the pioneers of an expressive modernism, Gunnar Birkerts) and worked in Chicago before coming to Las Vegas for a "change of scenery," expecting to stay there for only two years. The area's growth, as well as its surrounding natural beauty, made him stay there, and he currently lives not above, but next to the office and down the street from a coffee shop he owns in a small strip of three-story mixed-use buildings he designed in 2016.

The development is atypical for Las Vegas, but telling of Kimsey's ambitions and approach to making architecture there. Inspired by the density of Dutch row housing, Kimsey bought this small strip of land in downtown Henderson as part of an effort to revitalize what had been a working-class part of the valley. Many of the original art deco buildings were constructed as part of the building boom associated with the creation of the nearby Hoover Dam, while later buildings, presenting themselves with thin veneers of midcentury modern detailing, served factory workers and others not associated with the faraway Strip. As Las Vegas continued to sprawl, Henderson's outskirts turned into expensive suburban developments.

Kimsey saw the chance to help what is now an amorphous community regain its core. Using the small buildings to extend the scale and built-up character of the retail strip on Water Street, while also nodding to the stucco-clad, gable-roofed jumble of housing beyond, he designed two office buildings as cubical volumes and two residential structures whose base forms then rise up to the split and peaked roofs. In a manner that is typical for TSK's strategy, Kimsey accentuated windows with shadow boxes and added the orange stripes that are in some ways his signature to both horizontal and vertical elements. Stepping parts of the row of structures backward, while jutting other pieces out, he was able to create the sense of a complex of forms and uses within a simple—and affordably constructed—set of volumes. The urban mix is complex, even though both its component elements and its materials are simple.

Three Key Projects

The Water Street development is an updated and condensed version of the Clark County courthouse, which remains Kimsey's most notable addition to the Las Vegas' visual culture and civic life. Part of the success of this structure is due to the fact that court facilities are, due to the power of its judges, among the few governmental projects that have more adequate budgets. However, that very opportunity comes with a concomitant problem: those same judges often have pronounced design preferences. In this case, the building's greatest weakness, its rather muted palette of dusty reds and browns, is the result of their preferences.

While that coloration recalls the hues of expensive McMansions a bit too much, Kimsey was able to at least divide the wash into materials that range from a red sandstone around the central public areas, to a red concrete block for the base buildings that do not quite come forward to the street, and to integrate colored concrete for portions of the tower. He then went further in a decomposition of the mass than he has been able to in many of his other structures. The elevator shaft, itself pierced by a vertical fin and punctuated by square, recessed, and continuous windows on different faces, stands apart from the office and court block, which is itself a combination of concrete and glass assemblies and stucco walls. The tower roof caps the combination of elements as it rides over a slightly recessed top floor. The base, meanwhile, consists of a combination of volumes that come forward to address the different street frontages. A central atrium, expressed on the outside with the sandstone and an expanse of glass, signals the courthouse's public areas.

An even more expressive legacy building is the Springs Preserve nature center, a stack of rectangular and round elements nestled into an outcropping of rocks in another of Las Vegas' lesser known, working-class areas. The main structure, which acts as the visitor center, is a simple volume with few of the push and pull of elements Kimsey exhibits in other designs. Instead, the volume is broken up over its whole length by being an open grid filled in with Corten steel scrim. The structure rises as a bit of scaffolding out of its natural setting, sitting lightly within the expressive rocks and cacti while housing public functions that support the public's enjoyment and knowledge of that nature. The Ori-Gen museum, by contrast, consists of two rounded shapes around an atrium whose circular shape is clad with more of the Corten material. The central space erupts towards the visitor with another circle, in this case a canopy, sucking them into the exhibitions inside. This is one of the few places (outside of the firm's work in China) where TSK uses circular forms.

The public spaces and the entrance at the Springs Preserve also give a hint of what is another palette TSK and before that Tate & Snyder have used to give shape and identity to their larger structures, especially. It is particularly on display in the Harry Reid airport project. Both the terminal and the control tower are clad only in high-finish metal and glass, elevating their utilitarian, almost factory-like shapes to something that approaches the slickness of the airplanes circling around the buildings. Though this palette has now become dominant in airports around the world, Tate & Snyder was among the first to use it in 1998 to create their versions of airplane hangars for public use. Filled with natural light filtered by strong overhangs and opening up with vaulted roofs, the wings of the terminal also revolve around a circular atrium that, with its long escalators leading down to a tram station, acts as an eddy mixing and circulating passengers.

Breaking Boxes

In recent years, TSK's work has been split between the core activities in the Las Vegas office, and growing satellite operations in Southern California, Reno, and Shanghai. In each of those other locations the firm has developed different approaches, ranging from the manipulation of large commercial volumes in high-rise projects in China, to the adaptation of more rustic materials and looser plans in the Reno area, to an adoption of both Spanish Colonial and Southern California modernist elements for the Los Angeles commissions.

In Las Vegas, however, TSK has continued to develop structures that are seeking to compose the elements, traditions, and economic and cultural character of this very young metropolis toward a form of articulated coherence. Some of these, such as the new Student Union at the College of Southern Nevada in Henderson, represent the more expressive side of the firm's work, while others, such as the Sahara DMV Service Center, show the firm's ability to create beautiful civic spaces. It also still designs elementary, middle school, and high school prototype buildings, wresting moments of light and community spirit out of concrete block enclosures.

The Student Union is one of TSK's most expressive designs to date. It faces the main part of the campus with an acutely angled L-shape cowl, painted in Kimsey's favorite orange, over the main entrance. This entry leads to a corridor that acts as the space's main gathering space. Filled with indirect light, it is another of Kimsey's motifs: pack all the functions into spaces controlled and defined by those uses, and then save up enough circulation area to make what is left over into the most pleasurable, attractive, and memorable parts of the building. The public space's central portion is higher, creating an implied atrium lit through clerestory windows. The various service functions announce themselves to this street through blocks pushing in and out that are colored in bright hues, making the space a public and abstracted version of a mall. As in many other examples in TSK's work, the internal cave gives respite from the harsh climate and confused urbanism outside, setting up a place of gathering that is also a retreat.

This is one of the few of TSK's recent buildings that also has an open version of the entrance sign: a covered porch partially shaded by a scrim sliced diagonally toward an open tip The scrim continues around the corner to shade the dining area, while also serving as a larger way to signal the Student Union's identity toward the community around the campus. The rest of the building remains compact, but is still divided into blocks of different materials and colors, pushing and pulling at the volume to mitigate its scale and articulate the different functions it contains.

Against the snazziness of the Student Union, the Sahara DMV appears much more subdued. What you see on the outside is a collection of tightly packed utilitarian structures, the largest of which is a brick wall anchored at one end by a glass and corrugated metal block. A relatively small canopy of perforated metal pushes forward to emphasize the entrance at the intersection of the wall and the glass and metal volume. Look carefully, and you see that TSK eroded the bottom two-thirds of the wall to create a shaded space where the often long lines waiting to enter the building can stand. Thus the simple shed still offers a varied and accommodating aspect to the public. The letters "DMV" spelled out in oversized letters then mark the building's function, while a slow arched roof form indicates what awaits inside.

The payoff to that promise is the main space into which you enter after passing through the low vestibule. It is a large and simplified version of TSK's interior shelters. Clerestory windows under the arched roof provide lighting, while the transom above the offices is covered in wood. That is basically all there is to the space. Around it, the service kiosks, as well as vendors and a few work desks, fulfill the DMV's functions. The space is alive with activity, and yet peaceful. As an alternative to the usually fluorescent-lit boxes into which those waiting to obtain licenses usually have to wait, the Sahara DMV offers a much more humane version of basic government services. TSK is designing another DMV based on this design, a fact that also exhibits one of the firm's strategies: create a standard model that can be replicated, with variations, at minimal effect while containing as much good space as the architects can afford.

That approach is clearly on view in the George E. Harris Elementary School, which can stand in for the many such structures TSK has designed over the years and continues to produce. Truth be told, the outside of this and similar structures is not exactly inviting. Though the firm has, as usual, tried its best to break apart the large school's various components and create a composition that is both civic and friendly to its neighbors. Yet the school remains an inward-turned bunker constructed out of concrete blocks whose different colors and sizes only mitigate that defensive and economically driven attitude to a certain degree. Only the entrance pavilion, where an overhanging eave separated by a strip of windows from a blue tile wall also shelters a glass entrance, gives the building complex any sense of identity and openness.

It is on the inside of the school that TSK has once again made the greatest contributions to the institution. Its design work is most evident in the places of gathering, such as the auditorium (which also serves as a lunch room) and the library. Both of these are tall spaces, lit through a combination of clerestory windows and small punctures through the concrete block walls. Treated with a forthright clarity, they are boxes of light with thin metal columns and, in the case of the auditorium, a row of gables that breaks up their scale.

It is in the corridors that the firm has again wrested good space out of circulation needs. Although these connectors are just as bare-bones as the rest of the structure, TSK has used various methods to turn them into places where students can and might want to gather. Skylights punctuate what are sometimes two-story spaces. The second floor overhangs the first to create a sense of entrance for some of the classrooms. These can then open up into that captured space with roll-up garage doors, dissolving the barriers between the various classes and the community of the school. The sense of gathering is increased in one of corridors through the addition of an oversized staircase, clad in wood, which can also act as an impromptu auditorium or place for small groups of students to congregate.

The Harris school is typical of a large part of TSK's practice and how it approaches the difficult public tasks it faces. Working with the simplest and most affordable materials and the most forthright way of organizing a complex program, it breaks down the exterior as much as it can, creating compositions that are more in tune with both a human scale and the neighborhood. These assemblies also begin to make sense out of the jumbled urbanism of Las Vegas, while gesturing toward the boulders and other abstracted forms of the natural landscape. TSK delights in the industrial nature of this approach, looking back to the history of factory design, the optimism of midcentury modernism toward the ability to make a better world out of mass produced, human-made materials, and the elegance that can be found in a minimal approach to form-making.

Within these structures, TSK then creates shaded and yet light-filled shelters that act as internalized versions of the outside world. Here they push and pull at volumes as well, using the added freedom of different roof heights, sources of light, and changes in direction that come with any complex interior layout to heighten the effects of the multi-colored and -material blocks. TSK makes no effort to hide the basic nature and mass-produced quality of the building components, but rather celebrates them as raw elements that, with a lick of color and the sweep of a roof, can become parts of a varied and functional public realm.

Next Up

As TSK transitions to new leadership and ownership, it is also expanding the scope and nature of its projects. The Las Vegas Convention Center addition, by far the largest project it has worked on in terms of square feet, is indicative of the search for forms that move out from the angular, block-like compositions on which it built its compositions. It refers back to the ability of large hangars to become beautiful that it tested out at the airport, again through the manipulation of light and scale, but with a lighter and more expansive sense of public grandeur. The central atrium space is the where the architects' abilities sweep into view past an extended porch that also connects the building to rest of the complex. The exhibitions halls, meeting rooms, and break-out spaces all feed into that public arena.

In the Kirk Kerkorian education building at UNLV's medical campus, in the meantime, the firm is also experimenting with a larger budget that allows it to extend the push and pull of volumes and spaces. In a further boost to experimentation and complexity, the functions are more complex and have a greater emphasis on an array of places of gathering, learning, and meeting that obscure the borders between closed and open as well as public and private. TSK is here also able to use materials such as terra cotta and a complex window wall with built-in shading devices that create complex patters on the exterior and identify the structure's importance.

Windom Kimsey has been practicing in Las Vegas for forty years now, and the firms he has helped lead have developed strategies for making architecture in that social and physical climate that have been remarkably successful in creating some of the most decent, enjoyable, and civically appropriate buildings in the area. Yet TSK and its predecessors also stand for a larger family of firms in midsized metropoles around the world that are making their mark through the design of the institutions and facilities that give these urban areas a sense of place, meaning, and coherence. Though their designs, constrained as they are by budget and other factors, are not as experimental, expressive, or innovative as that of firms working in larger cities or with more moneyed clients, these designers are vitally important in making architecture that matters for these communities. Kimsey's and TSK's—and that of similar firms—contributions are legion, hard-won, and often beautiful, and they are worth both studying and valuing.

FIRM PROFILE

About

Since the founding of TSK in 1960, the firm has built a reputation for designing public projects of exceptional quality that are an integral part of the fabric of the communities we serve. We have always strived to create buildings that inspire and help shape the physical world in a thoughtful and lasting manner.

Heritage

TSK's roots go back to 1960 when George Tate founded the firm, George Tate and Associates. He was joined in 1974 by William Snyder who moved to Las Vegas from Pennsylvania. The name changed to Tate & Snyder Architects and the firm built a strong reputation designing public projects in Las Vegas. Windom Kimsey joined the firm in 1991 and became a partner in 1998. The firm evolved into Tate Snyder Kimsey Architects and expanded into the Reno | Tahoe area, and soon after the firm acquired Caldwell Architects in Southern California. Looking to the future the firm re-branded as TSK and expanded the leadership.

Future

Our firm's values are focused on designing buildings that serve their communities in responsible and innovative ways that are client focused. Our firm leadership has worked continuously to improve our services and capabilities to better serve our clients and provide an exceptional work environment for our entire team. In 2022, TSK became part of a larger consortium of architectural firms under the MORE Group, providing the firm additional resources, expanded capabilities, technological advances, and geographic presence to enhance our client services and reach new market areas. TSK will continue to look to innovative ways to enhance the client experience, support our talented team, and provide design excellence for the communities we serve.

"OUR PRACTICE IS GROUNDED IN THE BELIEF
THAT IDEAS EMBODIED IN A DESIGN SHOULD BE
PROGRESSIVE AND OF OUR TIME AND PLACE, THAT
SITE AND CONTEXT MUST PLAY AN INTEGRAL ROLE
IN THE BUILDING DEVELOPMENT AND THAT THE
SMALLEST DETAIL OF ANY BUILDING CAN BE JUST AS
IMPORTANT TO THE DESIGN AS LARGER AND MORE
APPARENT DESIGN LANGUAGE."

—Windom Kimsey, FAIA

Windom Kimsey
FAIA

Windom is president of TSK and he oversees the planning, development, and design of all projects. Since 1991, Windom has worked to enhance the quality of the firm's portfolio with projects that provide clients with exceptional design solutions. He has built a reputation for compelling, sensitive design, and has guided the firm to receive many prestigious honors, including over 100 design awards at state, regional, and national levels.

William Snyder
FAIA

George Tate handed over the firm's reins to Bill Snyder in 1982. Bill's leadership and vision helped shape TSK into one of the leading design firms in the southwest with an emphasis on educational architecture. Bill's enthusiasm and love of his adopted city laid the foundation for the firm's role in shaping Las Vegas and Southern Nevada. His passion for students resulted in Clark County School District naming an elementary school after him.

George Tate
AIA

The founder of TSK, George practiced architecture in Southern Nevada for more than forty years. His professional experience covered a broad range of project types and sizes, including many of the educational, religious, and health care facilities that continue to play significant roles in our community. The firm's business ethics and approach to teaming with its clients is firmly founded in the corporate culture created by George.

LEADERSHIP

Jason Andoscia
AIA

Wendy Sun
AIA, LEED AP bd+c

Mike Purtill
AIA, LEED AP bd+c

Shelly Lyons

Kevin Quan
AIA

Kevin Kemner
Associate AIA

Jeni Panars
AIA, LEED AP bd+c

Chris Lujan
AIA, LEED GA

Jonathan Richert
AIA

David Kim
AIA

Melanie Bailey

Kolby Harpstead
AIA

George Babakitis
AIA, LEED AP bd+c

Tom Lisciandra

Erica Bish
AIA

Adam DeCook
AIA

FIRM PROFILE: ACHIEVEMENTS

23

FIRM PROFILE: TEAM CULTURE

CURRENT

KIRK KERKORIAN MEDICAL EDUCATION BUILDING AT UNLV

Las Vegas, Nevada, United States | 2022

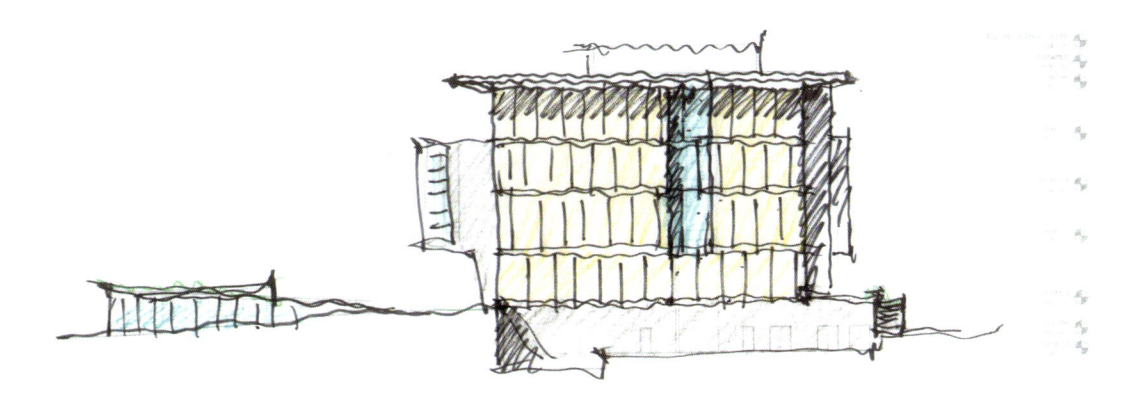

Despite years of explosive population growth, Southern Nevada has had a severe shortage of quality medical care. The Kirk Kerkorian Medical Education Building at UNLV represents a new era for medicine in the Las Vegas valley.

The proposed building is a 125,000-square-foot (11,613-square-meter) five-story structure, organized around strong circulation spines that help to connect students to the exterior and orient them to location in the building and the major building functions, which are *training*, *learning*, *community*, and *service*. The training floor serves as the building base and houses clinical skills, simulation, virtual and gross anatomy training programs. This "superfloor" of training spaces is unique in medical education and will distinguish the UNLV School of Medicine. The P-shaped superfloor is envisioned to be a concrete podium supporting the four-story tower above and provides opportunities for a secured outdoor gathering space. The community and learning spaces are concentrated on the second, third, and fourth floors, housing Student Life spaces, the Learning Studios, classrooms, and the library. Those administrative functions that serve the students directly, or are related to Admissions, are located at the top of the Forum on the third floor. The balance of the *service* functions of the building, the administrative offices, and dean's suite, are located on the fifth floor.

The massing of the building is oriented to maximize daylight and minimize direct solar gain with the integration of deep overhangs, brise-soleil, and strategic glazing placement. The strong horizontality of the desert is emphasized in the building massing through the organization of the building cladding and glazing components, in particular the horizontal ribbing of the terra-cotta panels, the inspiration of which is drawn from the jagged lines of EKG readouts. These panels also evoke the windswept sculpting of the walls at nearby Red Rock Canyon.

FIRE LANE

NORTH BUTTE
COUNTY COURTHOUSE

Chico, California, United States | 2015

A courthouse is an important and symbolic building for all cities. It is a tangible representation of our American ideals and represents the highest goals and standards of democracy. Throughout the design process, we looked to the history, landscape, environment and people of Chico and Butte County to create a distinctive facility that reflects Chico's unique culture and environment. An equally important obligation to the design was evoking the sense of reverence and dignity requisite for a courthouse in a contemporary yet timeless fashion.

The position of the courthouse creates a strong urban edge along the street with views looking out onto a proposed public park. The design intends to borrow this greenspace for use as a front yard to the building, enhancing its presence as a traditional place for civic gathering. The public entrance is on a raised plinth accessed by wide ceremonial steps, integrated seating areas, and sloped walkways, reflecting the historical tradition of American courthouse design and contemporary notions of accessibility for all.

The volume of the entry lobby rises above the roof plane. The light-filled space celebrates the sense of arrival, and its symbolism is deeply rooted in the notion of the courthouse tower on the town square—a glowing civic landmark at night. The large and welcoming roof overhang provides shade to the elevated pedestrian plaza and is supported by a series of large columns that reference the Greco-Roman historicism of important civic buildings in America and Western societies. The sleek and graceful columns reference a strong formality and civic presence that architecturally defines the building as a courthouse.

One of our primary design goals was to bring natural daylighting into as many spaces as possible throughout the building, including into the courtrooms themselves. North and controlled south openings allow daylight to enter and reflect off a light, billowing ceiling. A large overhang along the south façade protects against the harsh summer rays while allowing the warming winter rays to enter the space. High and large windows provide ambient light to penetrate deep into the north offices of the building.

Central to our design philosophy for civic structures are the qualities of dignity, strength, and permanence. We believe however, that strength need not exude harshness. The design for the North Butte County Courthouse strives to integrate warmth and transparency in a structure that both represents and serves the community it sits in.

TSK ARCHITECTS   CURRENT   42

B-TECH TOWERS

Shenzhen, Guangdong Province, China | 2018

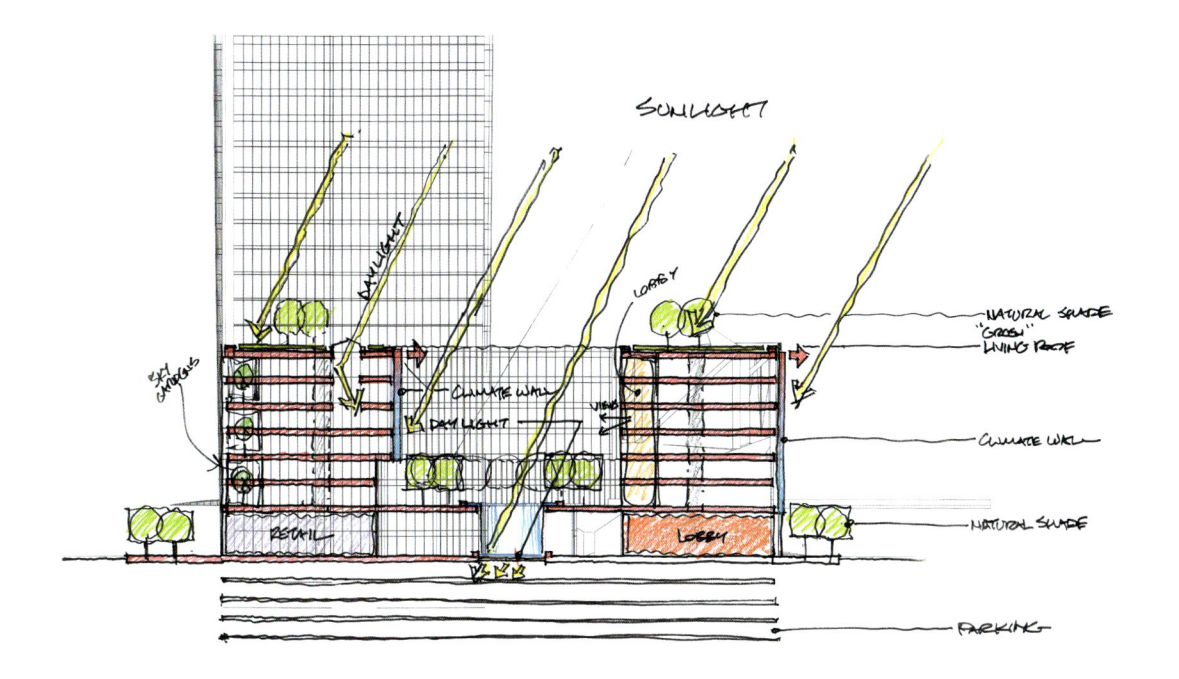

The Shenzhen Bay High-Tech Eco-Park in Shenzhen's Nanshan District is a planned development consisting of 18.8 million square feet (1.7 million square meters) accommodating R&D centers, headquarters of listed high-tech companies, and incubator centers for small/medium business innovation. The development is intended to serve as a platform for emerging industries of strategic importance, a national low-carbon industrial park, as well as a supporting center for the south zone of Shenzhen High-Tech Industrial Park.

The two 820-foot-tall (250-meter-tall) B-Tech towers are the tallest structures within the Shenzhen Bay High-Tech Eco-Park. They are the result of an international design competition and development process that was initiated in 2012. The lead architect, in collaboration with a local design institute, won the multiphase competition. The lead's role in the project consisted of concept, schematic, and design development as well as construction documentation review to maintain design integrity.

Echoing the "eco" theme of the planned development, sustainable strategies are integrated into the design of the two towers, consisting of 3.2 million square feet. The overall eco-park development is governed by a strict height restriction that led the design team to propose two slender towers rather than one large bulky mass. This allowed for design strategies that maximized daylight and connection to the surrounding landscape (viewsheds) influencing the shape of the towers resulting in the distinctive "splayed" massing. The twin towers are then positioned at opposing corners to further open sightlines and minimize self-shading. Natural ventilation is incorporated in the design through modular operable windows integrated into the façade system.

In addition to passive solar strategies, active solar strategies are implemented in the project as well and contribute to the building's performance. The project achieved a 2-Star Green Building rating under the ASGB Standard, equivalent to LEED Gold.

At grade, the towers are connected by a large podium base that is articulated so that the profile of the towers read as a continuous ribbon unifying the horizontality of the base with the verticality of the towers. The expansive glass façade of the podium provides panoramic views of Shenzhen as well as Hong Kong across the bay. The podium is programmed to include retail and commercial office space, with a luxury five-star hotel on the upper levels.

The B-Tech towers are situated among multiple public transport systems and sit above three levels of underground parking, enabling easy access to both public and private transit. From the pedestrian access at the northwest corner of the site, public traffic is directed to an open courtyard surrounded by shops and restaurants for personal and professional engagements.

The courtyard connects to the south and east of the sites through a green corridor, facilitating the easy transfer of pedestrian traffic to all the numerous surrounding functions. Through a series of landscaped plazas, visitors and employees are surrounded by food and retail kiosks that help enhance community engagement and interactions. A green roof space completes the design and provides a respite from the activity of the street and lower levels.

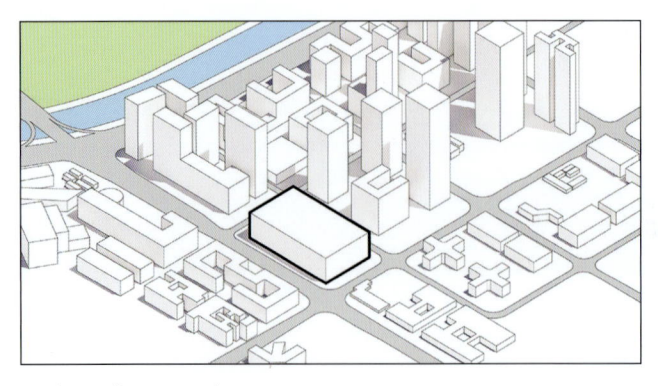

Basic podium massing

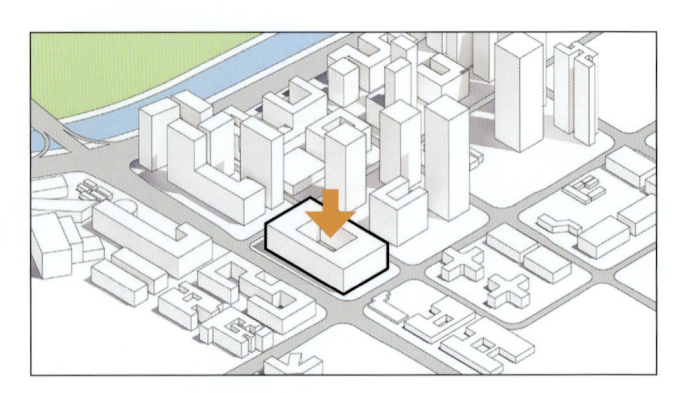

Open up the center as a courtyard to bring in the light and air

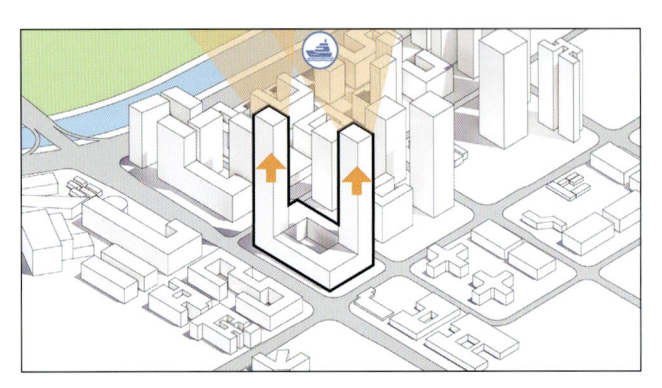

Raise the tower at the southwest and northeast corners for Shenzhen Bay views

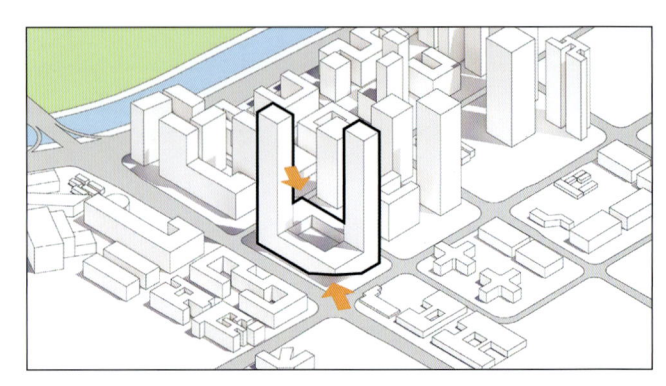

Lift the corner at southeast and northwest to make the entries more welcoming

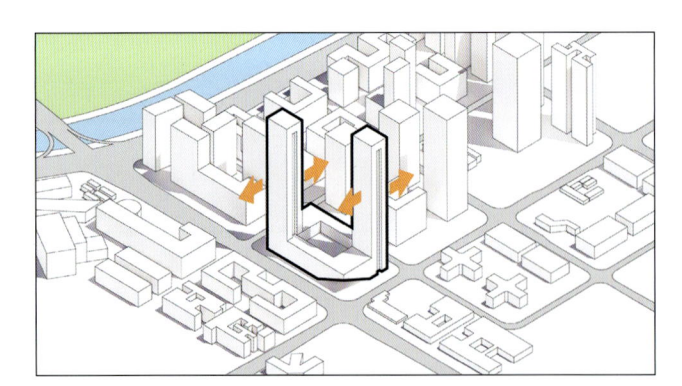

Move the tenant space to the south and north side of the tower to bring in the sunlight and view to the core

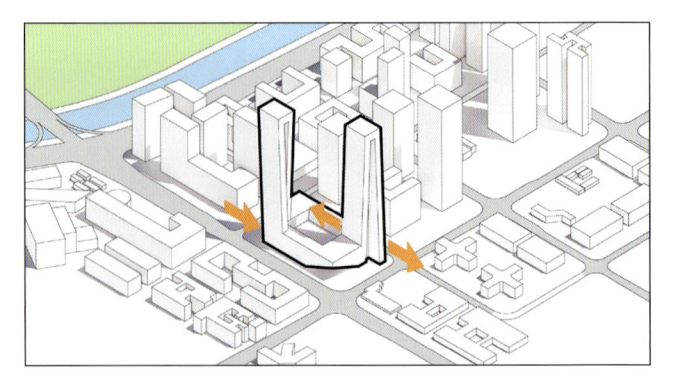

Angle the shape of towers to create more corner views from the leasable floor plans and invoke a sense of movement and rhythm

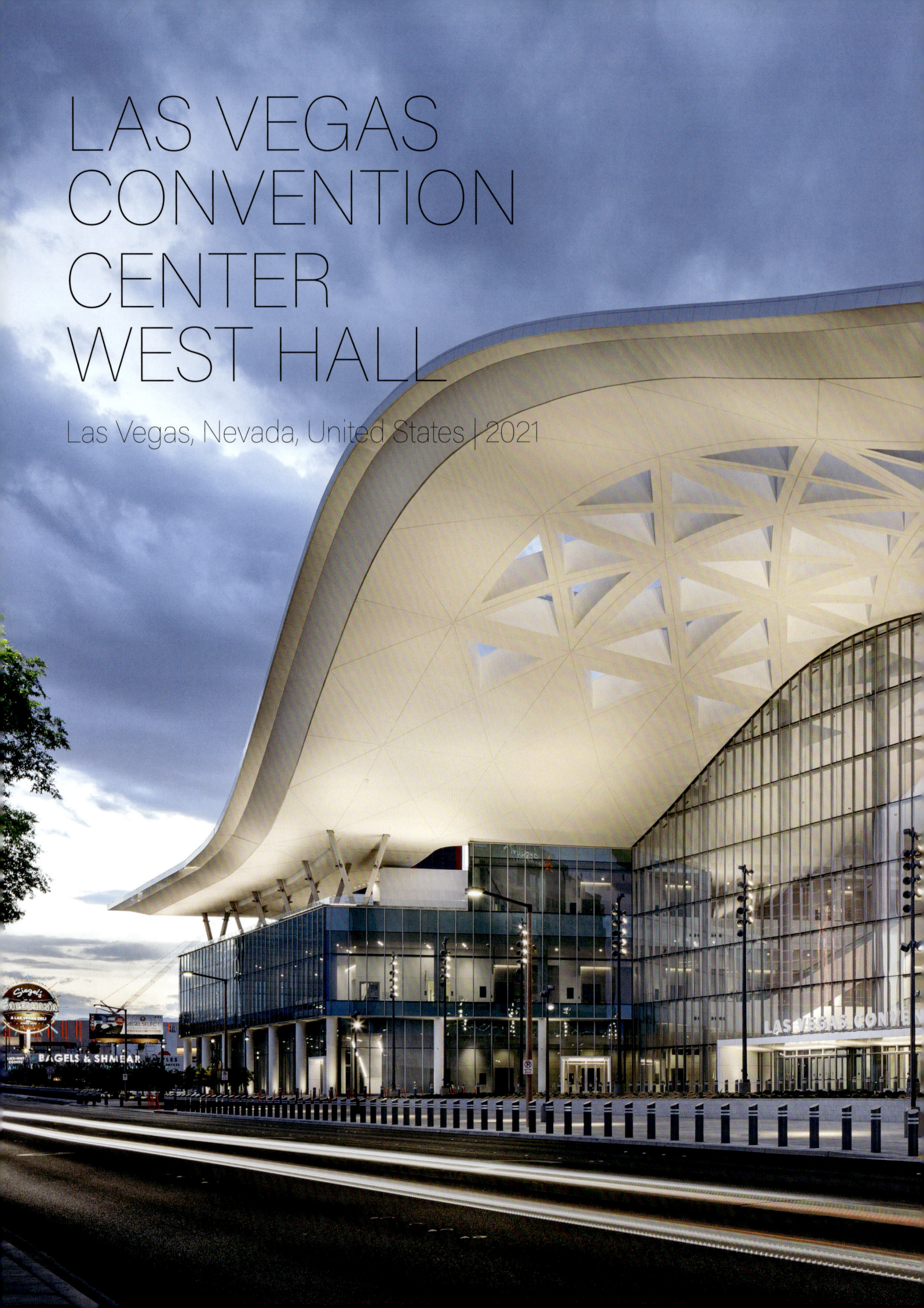

LAS VEGAS CONVENTION CENTER WEST HALL

Las Vegas, Nevada, United States | 2021

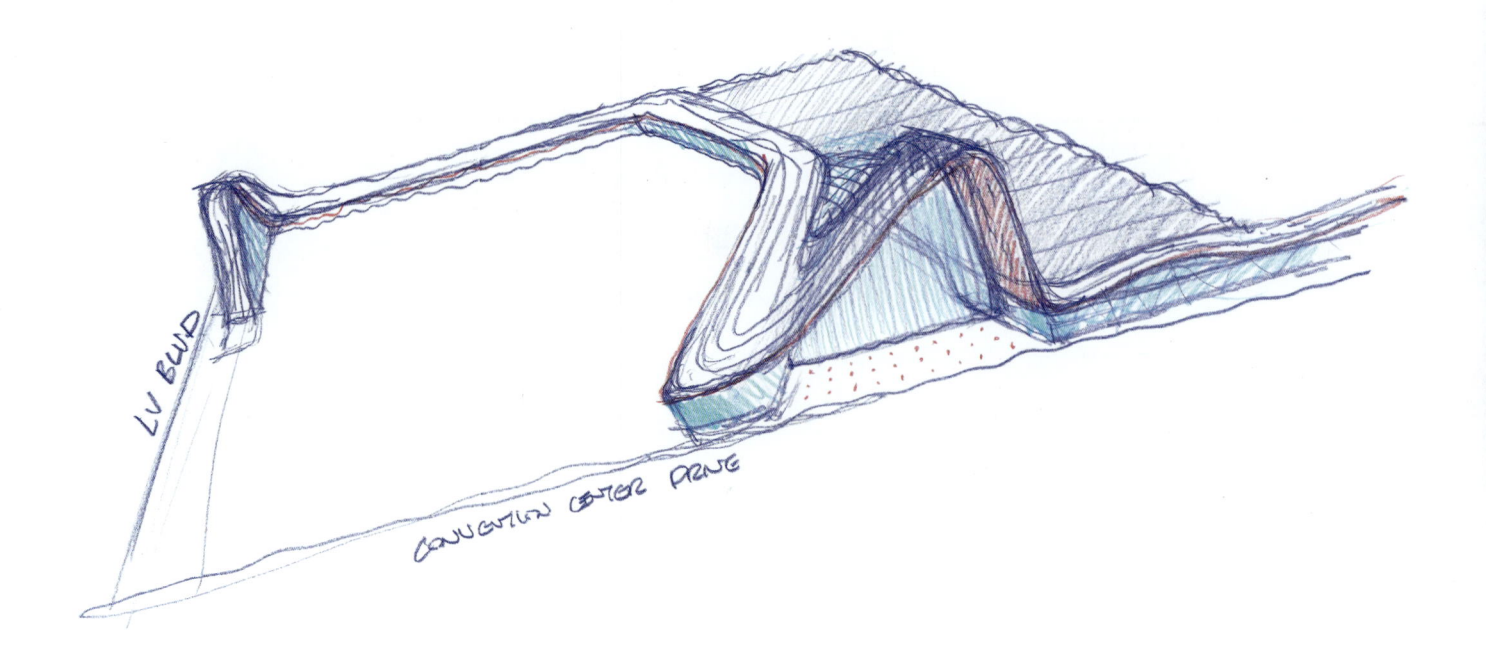

This project is the winning scheme for the design competition to create a major expansion and campus-wide upgrade to the Las Vegas Convention Center. The design team was a unique collaborative effort involving a team of five architects, bringing local, national, and international experience to create a design that captured the vision and brand of the Las Vegas experience, while at the same time fulfilling the complex functional requirements of the competition brief. This 1.44-million-square-foot (133,780-square-meter), fast-track project (budgeted at $860,000,000) hosted the 2021 CES convention.

The design begins with visual reach and experience that unifies the campus across the distance from the Strip to the South Hall. Access and program punctuate the campus between those two endpoints; nodes made cohesive by a "ribbon" of circulation. Echoing the region's mountains, the ribbon is amplified at significant points to unite, announce entry, and celebrate the act of gathering—an orienting path for the eyes, the feet, and the mind. The ribbon is a way-finding landscape of seamless connection and graphic activation from end to end, continuous and customizable to announce and activate the convention center and make it a visible player from Las Vegas Boulevard and its hotels; an artery of the Vegas experience piped straight from the Strip.

The design creates a compact, economical arrangement of program for the flexibilities that result from leaving much of the site open; an advantage for outdoor exhibits local to the Strip, for further expansion and response to surrounding development.

Programmatically, the exhibit hall is efficient and structurally repetitive, designed for steel construction speed to market unencumbered by surmounting structure or by scheduling dependencies of the adjacent concourses and conference center. Those are free to proceed on their own sequence in steel or concrete, however market influences advantage them. The circulation ribbon incorporates separate major lobbies so that separate entries can serve separate exhibit events in divided hall arrangements. The meeting program is stacked adjacent to the exhibit hall such that it functions in concert with exhibits or separately as an independent facility when the hall is unoccupied. It incorporates multiple spaces for inside/outside function.

Its circulation is organized to create and emphasize intersections and moments of rest for chance encounters. The competition was won through the design team's ability to collaborate and share ideas openly; testing the program and understanding the importance of this project to reinforce and enhance the city's brand in the world.

The design and execution of this facility came from an integrated team, including TVS Nevada Inc. as the architect of record with four local architectural firms: TSK, Simpson Coulter Studio, Carpenter Sellers Del Gatto Architects, and KME Architects.

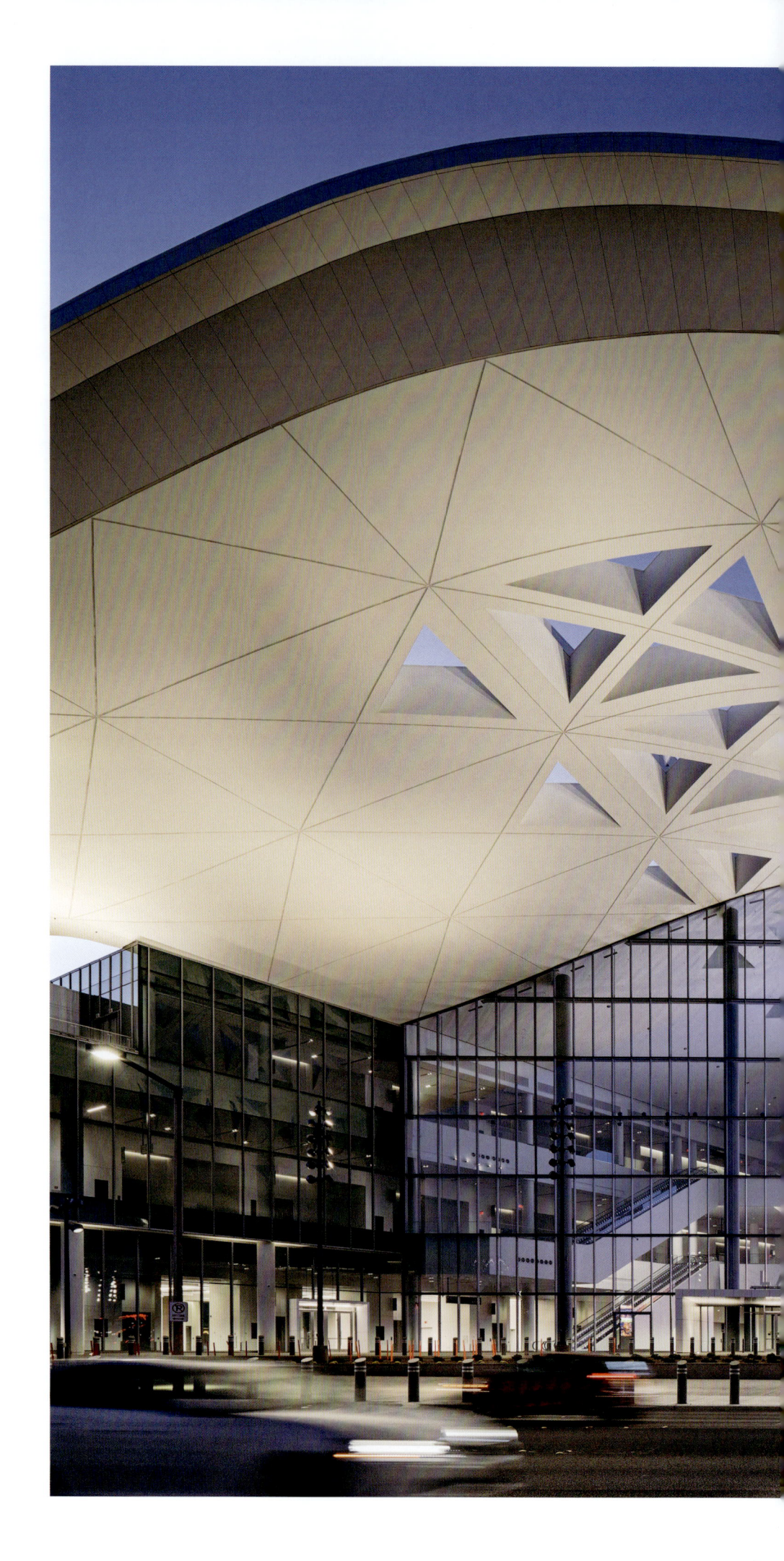

SILVERLAND
MIDDLE SCHOOL

Fernley, Nevada, United States | 2010

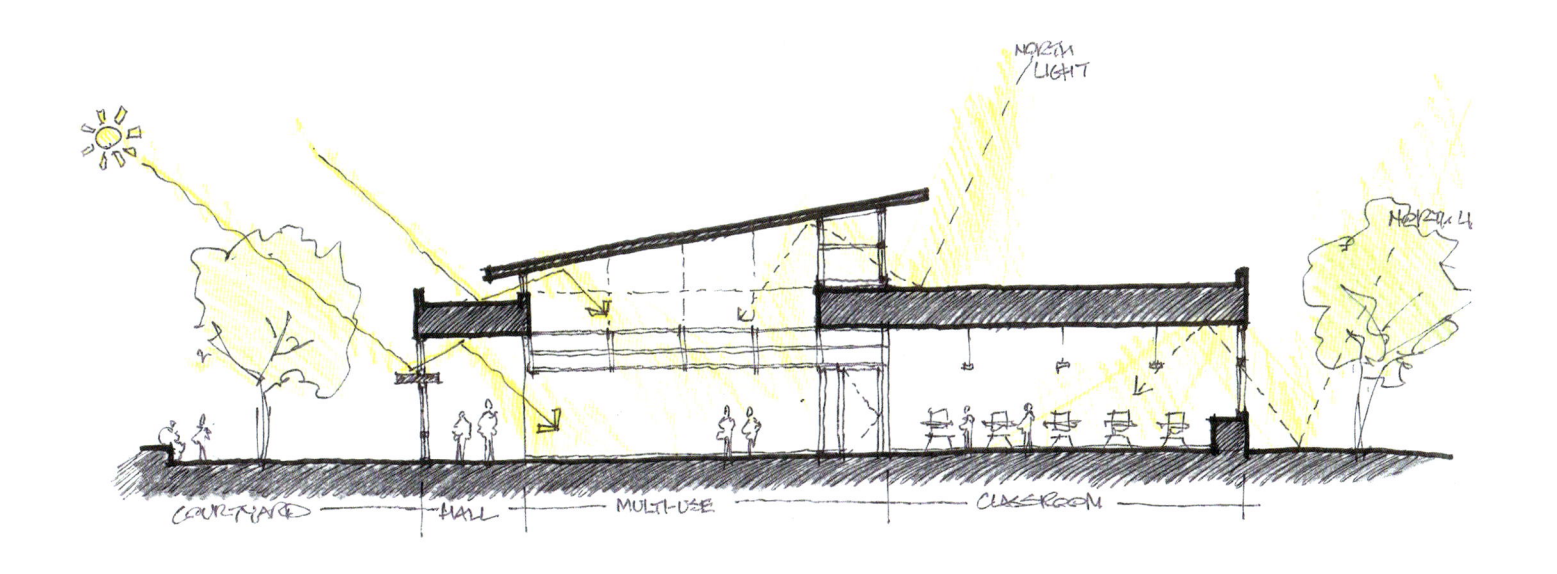

Completed for the Lyon County School District, we based the design of the intermediate school on grade-level wings that promote the notion of student neighborhoods and advance the practice of team teaching. The layout of the building circulation provides a functional connection for each wing to other destinations along the core of the school, such as computer labs, library, gymnasium, and performing and visual arts spaces. The central courtyard provides an essential age-appropriate space for student interaction, as it serves the needs of a flexible population and offers opportunities for community use during after-hours engagements.

Following a series of locally driven design charettes, we designed the new schools to respond to the needs of the community in both their programmatic and aesthetic arrangements. Developed as part of a new educational campus, the materiality of each school reflects both the local built and natural context of Fernley, while providing a sense of community and permanence.

Responding to budgetary limits, we integrated special materials such as glazed block, atlas brick, corrugated metal, and polycarbonate panels at special locations throughout each school. The exterior color palette of the campus reflects the cool colors associated with the fall and winter seasons. We juxtaposed these colors against a series of vivacious moments of color that code the various internal programmatic spaces, energizing the interior environment.

The school is oriented to maximize solar exposure from the south, while providing natural daylight to all classroom spaces. A solar hot-water system and series of wind turbines provide a renewable supplement to the energy demands of the campus.

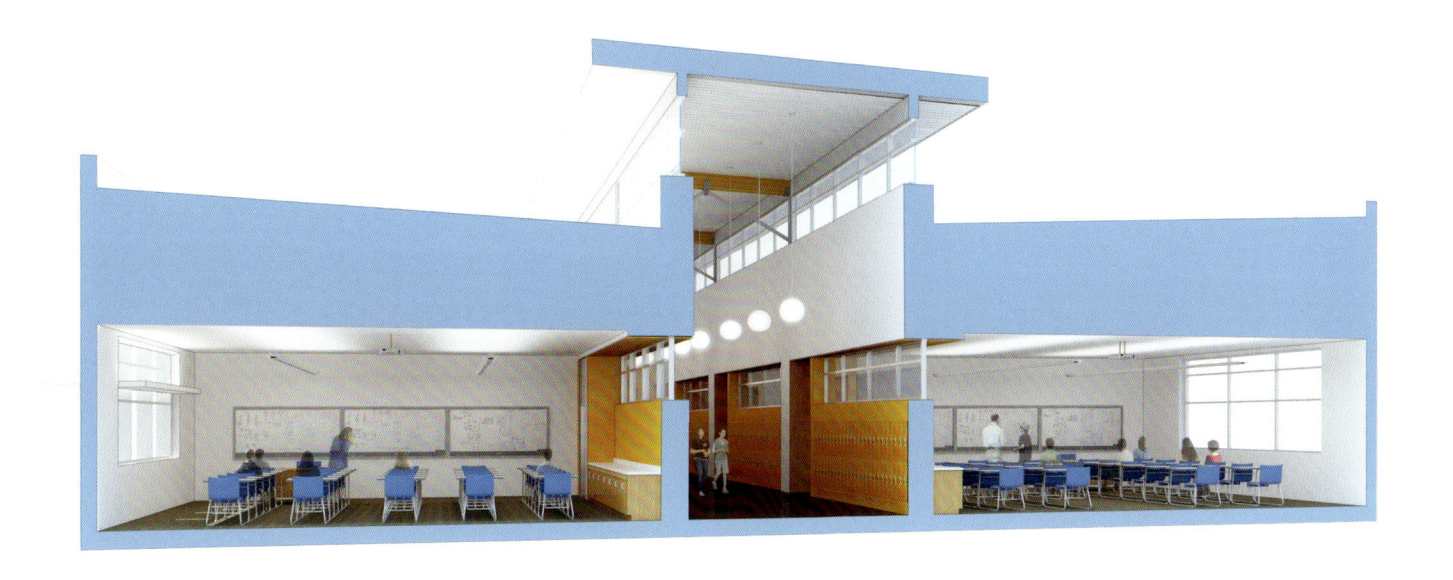

SOUTHEND ON WATER

Henderson, Nevada, United States | 2016–2022

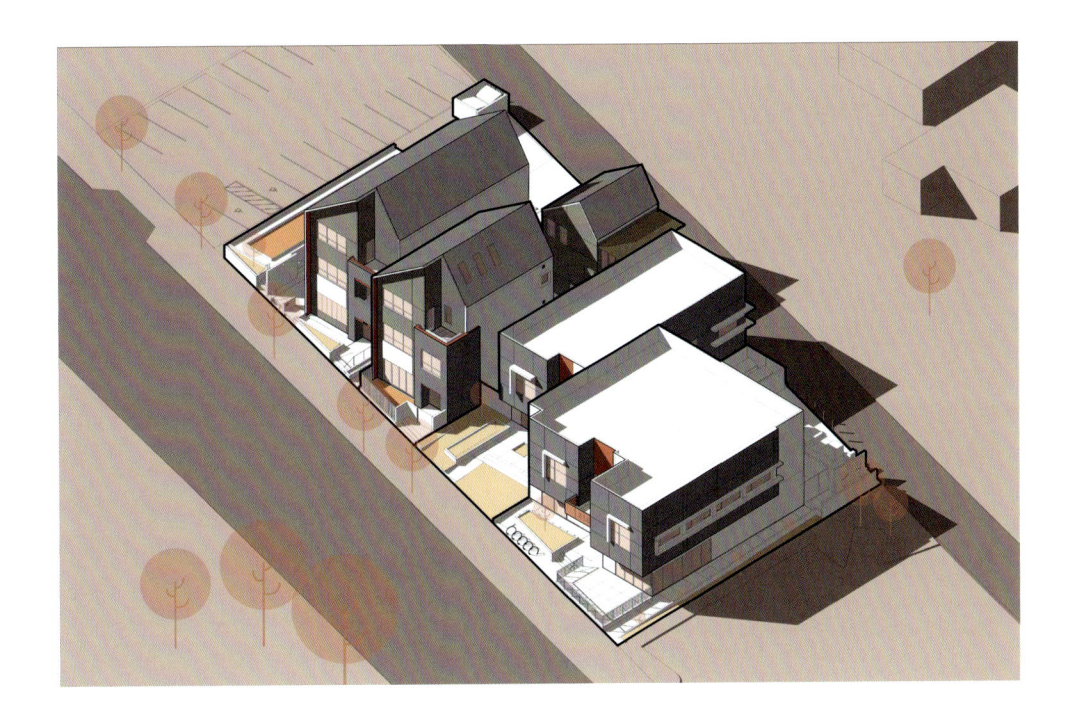

SouthEND on Water is a multiphased, mixed-use urban infill redevelopment in downtown Henderson, Nevada. It is part of the historic core of the city in the Water Street District. The genesis for this development was born out of a visioning charrette held by the City of Henderson to focus on redevelopment and revitalization of its downtown area. The architecture firm who helped facilitate the process determined that they would be an ideal candidate business for relocating downtown. This helped to kick-start the initial phase of SouthEND on Water, which has an architecture office and a coffee shop in a two-story mixed-use building. Utilizing the existing redevelopment grants available, the developer was able to build a project that provided office space and retail, creating a spark that has resulted in a wave of redevelopment downtown. Over the course of the next five years, constructed in four phases, the SouthEND development has now grown to include multifamily apartments, single-family housing, an Italian restaurant, additional professional office space, and a bocce ball court.

The project phasing occurred over five years due to the developer's incremental financing based on multiple city grants and land acquisitions. The commercial building is 11,000 square feet (1,021 square meters). The two-story structure addresses the street with massing that provides a direct connection for the coffee shop and allows pedestrians to see activity within the building. The architecture is modern and human-scaled to fit within the neighborhood. The materials are straight forward, utilizing finishes common to the region. The building massing is stepped to appear as two separate structures to reduce scale from the street and provides a forecourt in front of the offices that allows viewing of the two-story mural on the south façade. It also allows the flexibility to provide for future reorganization of the office and retail mix based on market demands.

The 3,600-square-foot (334-square-meter) three-story residential structures share an identical profile from the street and were influenced by Dutch housing typologies. One structure is a single-family home with an accessory dwelling unit over the garage, which is separated by a courtyard and connected by a second-floor bridge. It is elevated from the sidewalk and provides a usable set of stairs for seating during public events. The second residential structure is a mixed-use building with the Italian restaurant on the ground floor and an adjacent courtyard for exterior dining. The courtyard is enclosed by a set of offset walls that feature local artists' murals facing the bocce ball court. Above the restaurant are three apartments with balconies facing Water Street. All the structures share a common palette of materials and colors that integrate the overall design. SouthEND on Water has become an important catalyst for the city and for developers to invest into the downtown core.

SAHARA DMV
SERVICE CENTER

Las Vegas, Nevada, United States | 2016

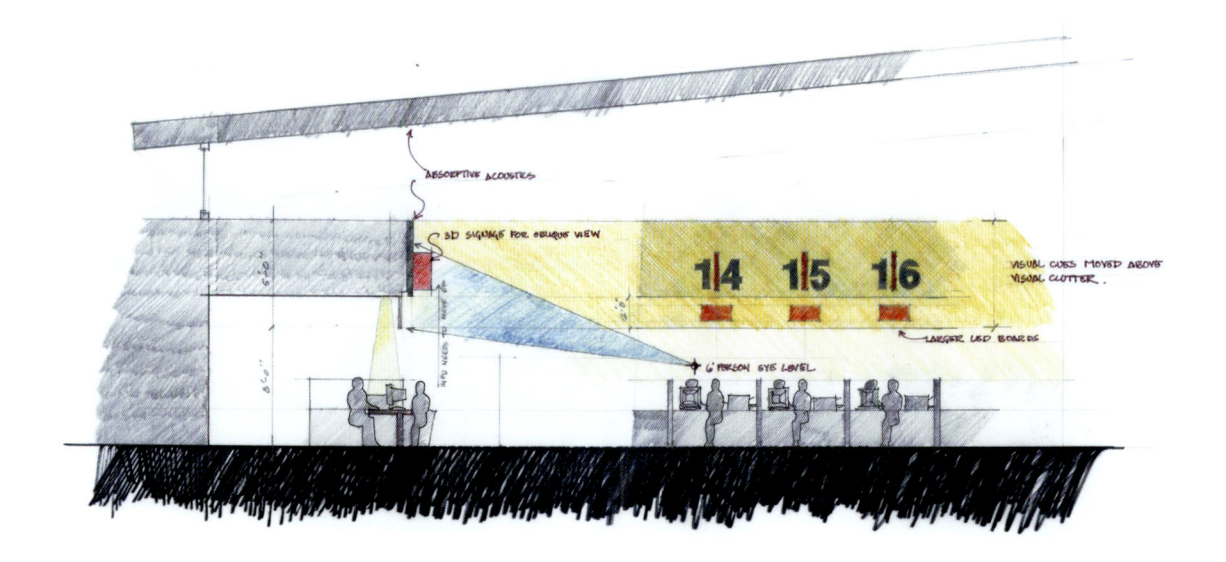

In 2012, TSK created the master plan and designed a new replacement facility for the Nevada Department of Motor Vehicles that helped modernize the DMV operations and which served as the prototype for future facilities. The 41,284-square-foot (3,835-square-meter), single-story facility is sited on 11.5 acres (4.65 hectares). The building plan and site organization work together to efficiently support customer movement, service access, visibility, and employee safety. The high-volume lobby space is the centerpiece of the facility, accommodating 2,000-plus visitors per day and up to 400 visitors at any one time. The height of the lobby serves multiple objectives: It relieves the sense of crowdedness during heavy business hours, and it helps with customer wayfinding by providing space for signage to be mounted above eye level. Given the high levels of stress DMV customers often feel during their time in these facilities, several steps were taken to use environmental design to improve the customer experience. While the perimeter of the lobby is largely occupied by customer service functions, the design takes advantage of the large clerestory to bring in filtered natural light, which works to reduce customer and staff anxiety. Nevada's DMV service centers tend to be noisy, which adds to the stressful environment. The Sahara DMV incorporates high levels of sound absorptive material to mitigate echo and noise amplification, significantly calming the space.

COLLEGE OF SOUTHERN NEVADA STUDENT UNIONS

Henderson, Las Vegas, and
North Las Vegas, Nevada, United States | 2019

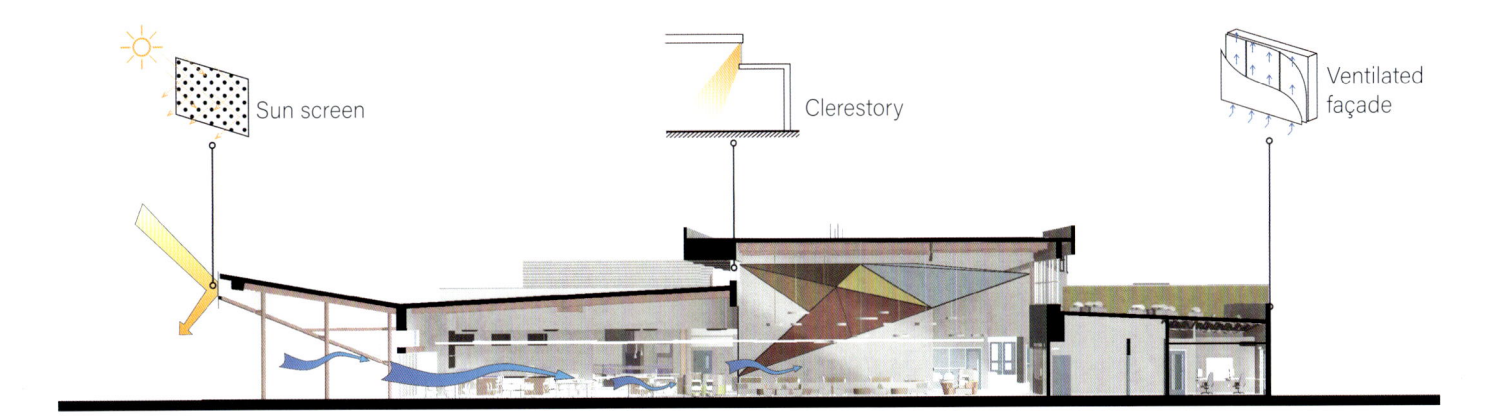

Sun screen · Clerestory · Ventilated façade

The College of Southern Nevada (CSN) presented our design team with a unique challenge for the design of a prototypical student union building to be constructed on each of the college's three campuses simultaneously. The students did not have a place where they could gather, study, work on group projects, relax, and enjoy a meal, or simply have a place to spend time between classes.

Our primary considerations in designing this facility were solving the above concerns, while enhancing the campus and student culture experience by achieving the following goals: simplify on-site circulation; define the main entry; provide transparency between the commons and exterior/campus; create comfortable space for students to gather; daylight the high-volume and internal spaces, including the commons, main corridor, and meeting rooms (controlled); provide meeting space with access to the exterior, pre-function space, and to the kitchen for catering purposes; clad the building in durable materials; and design a building that would be the focal point of the campus.

The proposed building was a 28,887-square-foot (2,684-square-meter) single-story building with a high-volume commons and food service seating space. Primary considerations in the design of the facility are student flow, access to food services and student services (Advising; the student government group [ASCSN]; Multicultural), functionality and access to the meeting rooms, and providing a comfortable place for students to gather, as well as a focal point of each campus. We worked closely with CSN's planning and construction department along with the building user groups, including student services, student affairs, diversity and multicultural affairs, events planning, purchasing (food service planning), and, most importantly, the students themselves through their student government group.

The student union incorporates several strategies to not only provide an energy efficient building, but also provide a pleasant space for students and employees. The strategies we employed: an energy management control system; displacement ventilation system at the meeting rooms; LED lighting with daylight dimming; fan wall technology plus high-application chillers/coolers; roof-top mounted photovoltaic panels; high-efficiency plumbing fixtures; daylight-diffusing glazing at clerestories; low VOC recycled content materials; and cool-roof technology. By incorporating these strategies, the energy use for the design is predicted to be 39 percent better than the baseline. These renewable energy strategies are anticipated to produce 40 percent of each building's energy use.

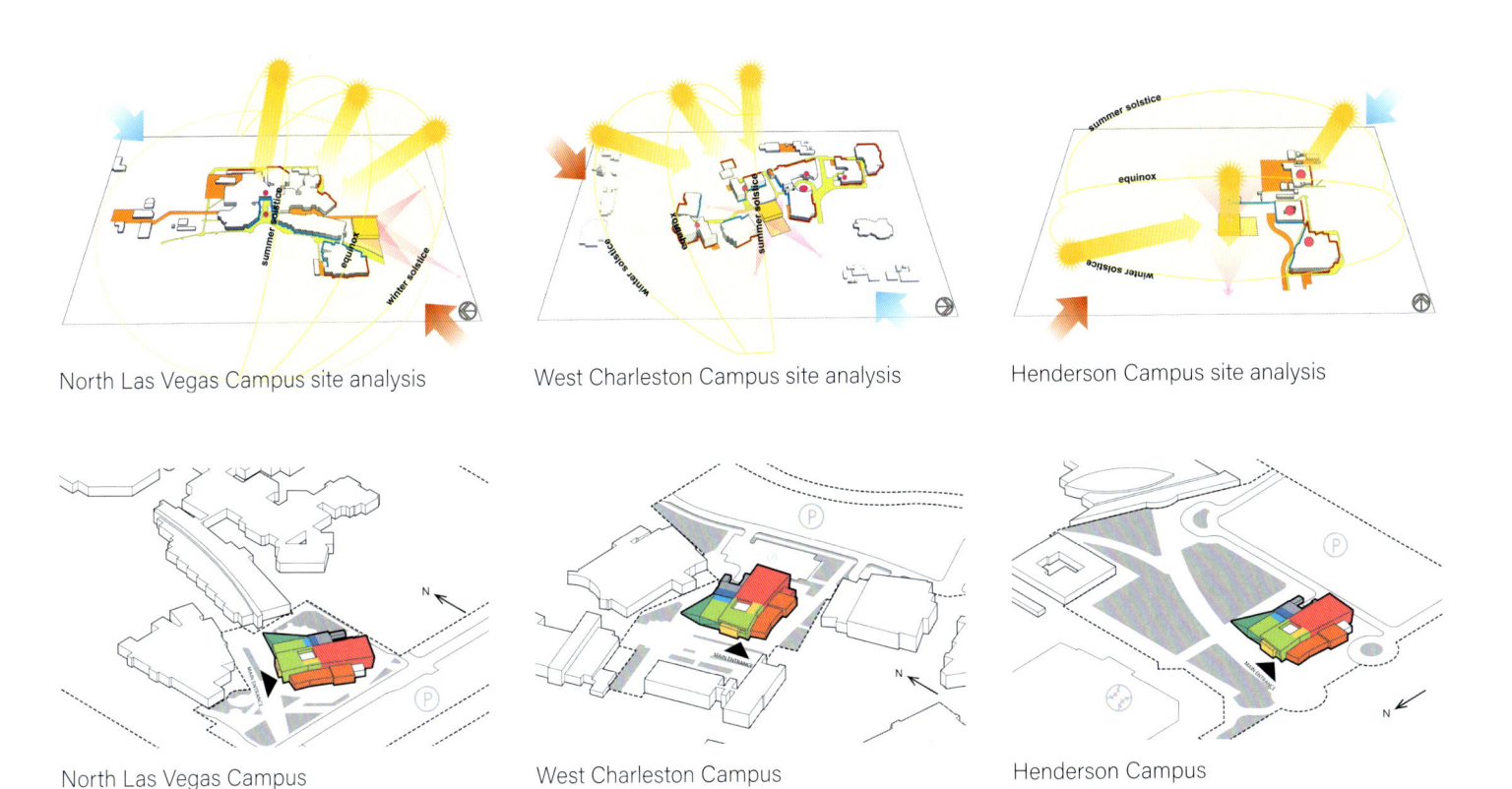

North Las Vegas Campus site analysis

West Charleston Campus site analysis

Henderson Campus site analysis

North Las Vegas Campus

West Charleston Campus

Henderson Campus

Centralized gathering areas provide opportunities for engagement and social interaction, which promote the holistic goals of campus life activities

REX BELL ELEMENTARY SCHOOL PROTOTYPE

Las Vegas, Nevada, United States | 2017

Evocative of a time in which Las Vegas gained early notoriety as a destination for both locals and celebrities to share in newly established neighborhoods in an otherwise desolate community, the Rex Bell Elementary replacement school celebrates the memory of place through a variety of design considerations. The new Rex Bell Elementary School seeks to continue the legacy of its 1964 predecessor and is to remain a tribute to its namesake. Named after the celebrated actor and noted politician, Rex Bell, the replacement facility will recall an era in which he was most active through subtle design references to midcentury modernism.

The new elementary school is located on the previously undeveloped approximately 2.8-acre (1.1-hectare) grass play area to the east of the existing building. The building consists of two stories: Level one is 73,965 square feet (6,872 square meters) and Level 2 is 27,103 square feet (2,518 square meters), for a total of 101,304 square feet (9,411 square meters) and was constructed on the existing active campus. The scope of work included site improvements, as well as the new parking areas, curb cut realignments, playgrounds and equipment, and a bus drop area. New construction, demolition, and removal of existing site amenities and buildings were phased in order to keep the existing operations uninterrupted for the school year.

Providing a safe and vibrant learning environment was of primary concern for our design team. Given the on-going challenges present in the neighborhood surrounding the site, a unique strategy for the building massing allowed for a series of internal activity areas, which are not impacted by such external challenges. After hosting a multiday design charette with teachers, staff, students, and community members the design team presented an overall design concept that would serve as

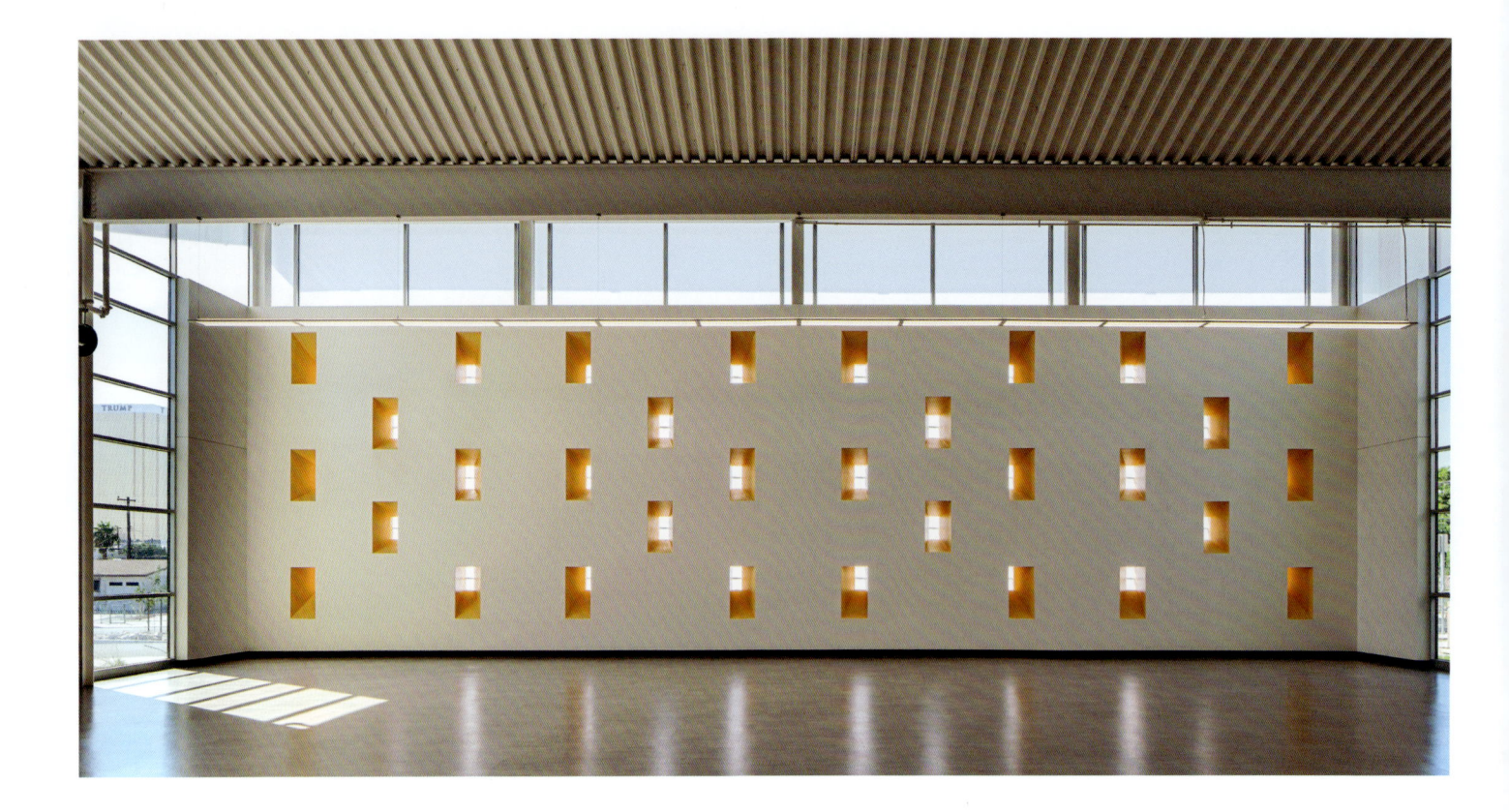

the basis of our collective vision for the school. The design allowed for the school to provide elevated views to the Strip, thus ensuring a lasting connection to the community and areas beyond.

Beyond providing insular classrooms and standard learning environments our design team sought to advance the character and function of otherwise neglected spaces. As such, the main circulation corridor along the northern portion of the facility was expanded without impacting the overall area. Core functions were moved into the center of this zone and thus provide for a wider interior that serves as both an area for circulation and breakout educational opportunities. This zone is oriented from east to west and benefits from a series of large skylights that provide daylighting throughout the space. Furthermore, the organization of the building program creates courtyards that serve as special outdoor learning environments for programs, such as the school's garden-to-table program and the kinder play area.

Collectively, these deliberate gestures support the overall goals of the design team while addressing the requests of those who participated in the charette. This facility successfully situates itself on an existing site and allows for the construction process to occur without interruption to the existing buildings on-site.

Rex Bell Elementary School is used as a prototype to develop other elementary schools in the Clark County School District, such as J.M. Ullom Elementary School, George E. Harris Elementary School, Gene Ward Elementary School, and Harley Harmon Elementary School.

LINCOLN ELEMENTARY SCHOOL PROTOTYPE

North Las Vegas, Nevada, United States | 2017

Reflecting the generational changes that have occurred throughout the neighborhood anchored by the Lincoln Elementary School since 1963, the design for this replacement facility celebrates the rich tapestry of cultural identities of its diverse residents while recognizing the link this site will forever share with the nearby Nellis Air Force Base following a tragic air crash in 1964. The integration of vibrant colors seeks to set this space apart from the otherwise neglected surrounding landscape of the neighborhood.

Providing a safe and vibrant learning environment was of primary concern for the design team. Given the on-going socio-economic challenges present in the neighborhood surrounding the site, a unique strategy for the building massing allowed for a series of internal activity areas that are not impacted by such external challenges. After hosting a multiday design charette with teachers, staff, students, and community members the design team presented an overall design concept that would serve as the basis of our collective vision for the school.

Beyond providing insular classrooms and standard learning environments our design team sought to advance the character and function of otherwise neglected spaces. As such, the main circulation corridor along the northern portion of the facility was enhanced without impacting the overall area. Core functions serve as a buffer to this zone and further isolate sound transmission between the classrooms and corridor, thus providing a more dynamic interior that serves as both an area for circulation and breakout educational opportunities. This zone is oriented from east to west and benefits from a series of large roof monitors, which provide daylighting throughout

the space. Furthermore, the organization of the building program creates both public and private courtyards that serve as special outdoor learning environments and community spaces. The main entry lawn serves as a community lawn in a neighborhood that lacks such informal spaces—a reality that is not uncommon in this region.

Collectively, these deliberate gestures support the overall goals of the design team while addressing the requests of those who participated in the charette. This facility successfully situates itself on an existing site and allows for the construction process to occur without interruption to the existing buildings on-site which needed to remain operational.

The new Lincoln Elementary seeks to continue its legacy as a central destination in the neighborhood since 1963 and provide needed learning and activity spaces for the community. Earl N. Jenkins Elementary School, located on the east side of the Las Vegas Valley, is also developed based on this Lincoln Elementary School prototype.

CXTX
AUTO CITY
PHASE II

Kunming, Yunnan Province, China | 2021

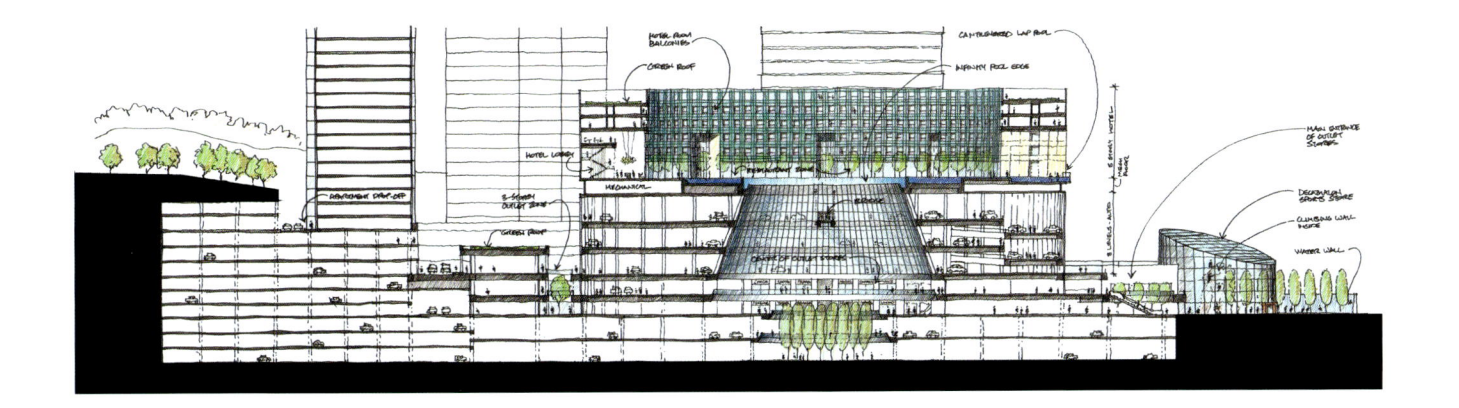

We have been working with Runsun Development Group on CXTX Auto City.

Phase II is a mixed-use development based on an automotive theme. The 3,700,000-square-foot (343,741-square-meter) project consists of dealerships, a used-car center, a new car exhibition showroom, retail, cafeterias, a 492-foot-tall (150-meter-tall) office tower, hotels, resorts, and two apartment towers.

The design is based on the characteristics of a hillside village. Winding roads with shops on both sides remind people of charming Italian mountain villages. Winding roads are not only pleasant to walk but also interesting to drive. The road is designed to fit the human scale. The bridge that connects both sides on the upper floor activates the space, thus becoming a focal point and a viewing platform.

TOPAZ

Los Angeles, California, United States | 2018

Topaz is a mixed-use urban infill project located in the historic core of downtown Los Angeles with 159 apartments and 23,000 square feet (2,137 square meters) of retail. The site borders the Toy District to the east and Historic Core to the west and presents two very different contextual opportunities. Our design concept was to respect the adjacent historic buildings by continuing the rhythmic elements into the new façade and maintaining the street wall.

On Los Angeles Street, the building is oriented to optimize solar exposure in the courtyard through an urban window with a light curtain that is designed to maintain the street wall, buffer the harshness of the warehouse district, and light up at night to provide a sense of safety and visual interest.

On Main Street, the historic building to the south has a motor court that is preserved and provides an opportunity for a corner exposure in the direction of a one-way street. The design respects the classic base, middle, and top organization, with dramatic emphasis on the corner and top of the building with a contemporary rendition of a classic blade sign found throughout the historic core of Los Angeles.

CLARK COUNTY FIRE STATION NO. 61

Las Vegas, Nevada, United States | 2021

The daily demands placed upon first responders and firefighters require the facilities that serve them to be robust and adaptable. Fire stations are designed to meet the needs of the staff, agency, and the community that it serves. The Clark County Fire Station No. 61 is a replacement to the existing Station No. 16, which was built in 1979 and is no longer able to serve the operational needs of the Clark County Fire Department. Since 1979 the surrounding community has grown into a diverse and vibrant district anchoring the east side of Las Vegas. The otherwise modest facility will be replaced by a structure that evokes pride and identity along a busy thoroughfare at the center of this community.

Following a series of site investigations and departmental evaluations of other recent fire stations, this new facility seeks to enhance the daily live-work staff experience. The design team was considerate of budget limitations and sought to use materials that were reflective of elements commonly associated with firefighting. Furthermore, issues related to staff safety, health and wellness, and comfort helped to inform our design decisions.

The project includes three apparatus bays and the shared living areas—which include a central kitchen and dining area, captains' living quarters, exercise and fitness room, day room and twelve private sleeping quarters—are planned around a central outdoor living space. Consideration of the separation between the apparatus bay and living areas was critical to limiting the firefighters' exposure to chemical contaminants and noise. The layered mix of private and common areas throughout the building enables opportunities for individual staff members to seek privacy when needed and re-engage the team without creating zones of isolation.

CLARK COUNTY FIRE STATION NO. 61

U.S. BUREAU OF RECLAMATION DATE STREET CAMPUS

Boulder City, Nevada, United States | 2011 & 2013

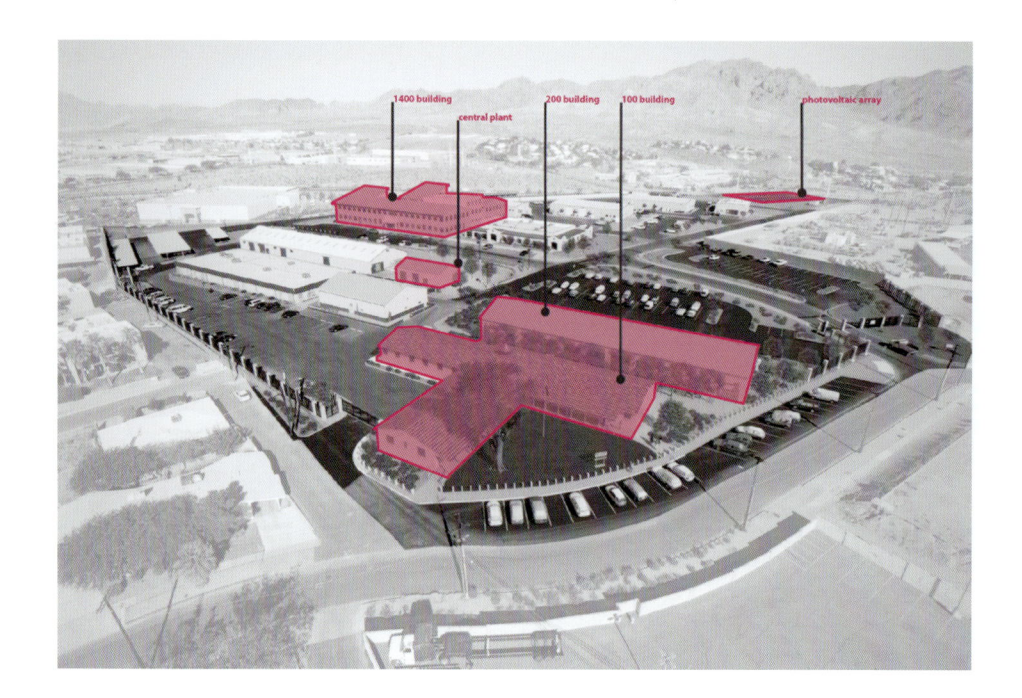

TSK has worked with the U.S. Bureau of Reclamation in Boulder City, Nevada, at its historic Date Street Campus since 2011. In that time, our team has master planned the campus, designed over 100,000 square feet (9,290 square meters) of new construction and renovation spaces (many of which are included on the State's Historic Register), and designed over 10 acres (4 hectares) of site improvements.

Redevelopment of the former Bureau of Mines campus began with the Lower Colorado Regional Office Building (Building 1400). The 49,000-square-foot (4,552-square-meter), two-story contemporary office building draws on precedents from the historic buildings on the campus and merges characteristics of the existing architectural styles, as recognized in Building 100 (the original 1941 Bureau of Mines Administration Center and Laboratory) and Building 200 (the original 1931 vehicle repair garage for Six Companies, Inc. as it constructed the Hoover Dam). Collectively, the design solutions respect the historic neighborhoods surrounding the campus and while recalling the historic industrial themes.

The interiors reflect the bureau's rich history in the Lower Colorado River region using stylized historic imagery of the Hoover Dam construction throughout the space as wall graphics, gabion walls filled with tailings from the mountains blasted away from the Black Canyon to make way for the dam, and a mosaic from regional core drilling samples. These details fuse the legacy of the agency into the architecture of the space. The building attained LEED Platinum level certification and achieved net zero energy consumption after the Phase II solar farm installation. Principles of daylighting incorporated provide 80 percent of the spaces to be daylit and more than 90 percent of the occupants to have direct views to the outside.

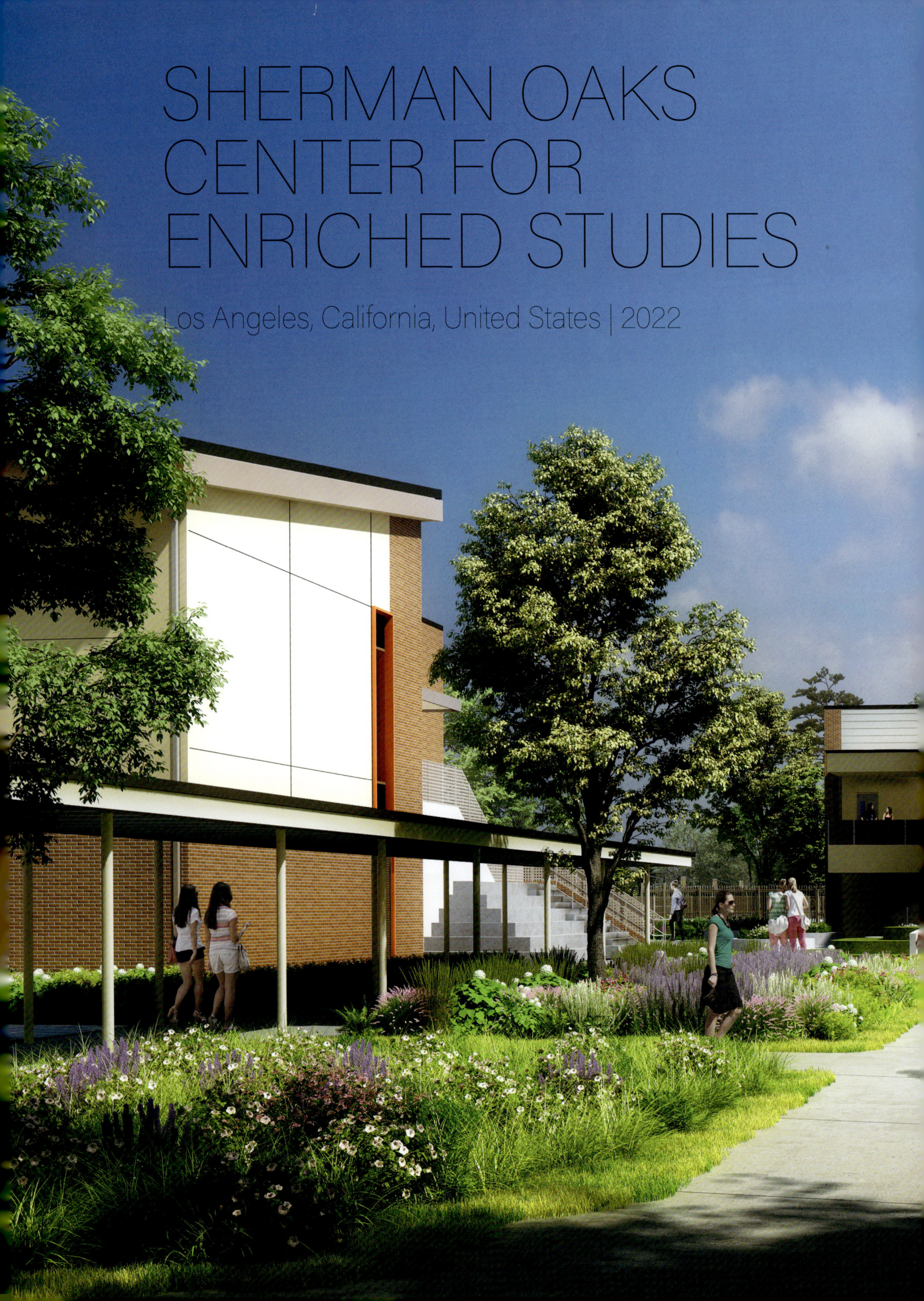

SHERMAN OAKS CENTER FOR ENRICHED STUDIES

Los Angeles, California, United States | 2022

The overall design concept of the campus is based on the simplicity of form in the existing historical layout and architecture of the campus. The proposed campus re-establishes the center of campus at the Center Circle, balancing the existing radial finger classrooms layout at the east with the more formal, clustered layout at the west. The addition of a student center plaza at the north, a student quad at the west, and small activities courtyards at the east promote individual, focused activity nodes beyond the Center Circle. The existing walkway element throughout the campus inspires the emphasis of outdoor walkway connections within the new classroom buildings.

The existing school structures were designed in simple modern styles where new buildings adopted these features but added playfulness and sculptural forms, thus creating a basis of design language for future expansions.

New buildings are sensitive and compatible to the scale, form, and proportion to existing one-story buildings. Character-defining features, such as simple rectangular massing, shed roofs, and brick façade accents, are adopted onto the new buildings.

Overall, the new buildings take the simple modern building layout and forms of the existing classroom buildings to create a campus blend. The materials were chosen carefully for durability and ease of maintenance. The circulation is logical and simple. The design takes advantage of the natural light available to create a bright and cheerful environment for the students both inside and outside. These campus additions will help further the successful mission of Sherman Oaks Center for Enriched Studies campus for twenty-first century learning.

JOHN F. MILLER
SCHOOL

Las Vegas, Nevada, United States | 2013

In 2011, the Clark County School District awarded TSK (in collaboration with Core Construction) the first design-build school for the district. The new John F. Miller School replaced the existing facility that serves a special community in the Las Vegas area. The school provides special education programming and services for students with specialized needs for ages three to twenty-two years. The school's motto is that all children can learn. It is committed to providing all children with the opportunity to reach their maximum potential while preserving their dignity and treating them with respect.

The design of this school supports this mission. All students have individualized education programs that reflect their unique and specialized needs. Each classroom allows for highly flexible layouts, providing the staff with unique opportunities to participate in a wide range of teaching environments. Classroom spaces, as well as corridors, are daylit using translucent panels and are organized around courtyards that interrupt the building mass. This allows for sheltered outdoor areas for exploration and relaxation. Distinctive to this school is a centralized health center that provides medical assistance to each student's specific needs. This component allows for a unified experience supporting both education and well being.

The scope of work meets the functional requirements of the school, with a new 68,875-square-foot (6,399-square-meter) building plus associated site work that includes twenty-two classrooms, health center, physical education space, multipurpose room, library, administration offices and conference/training rooms, and building systems support spaces. TSK designed the site to incorporate a raised bus platform at the same elevation as the school itself, allowing students ease of access without the need for lifts and ramps.

TRUCKEE MEADOWS
FPD STATION NO. 33

Reno, Nevada, United States | 2018

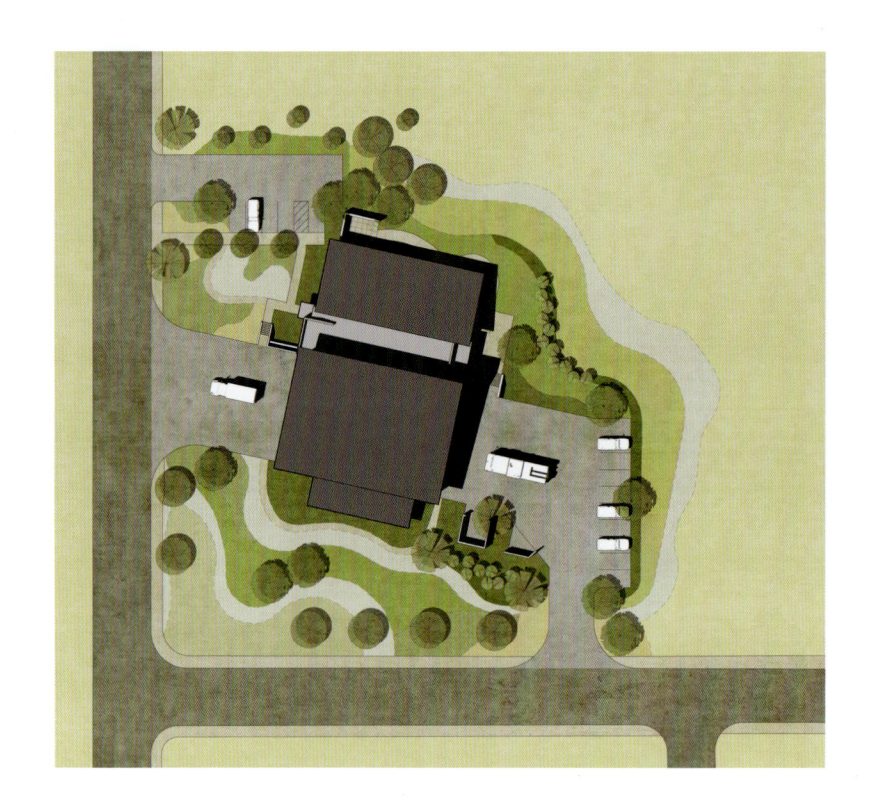

Truckee Meadows FPD Station No. 33 replaced an existing station that was no longer capable of serving the needs of the Truckee Meadows Fire Protection District (FPD). The previous site was located in a largely undeveloped region of the southern valley. Over the years, however, this location has become annexed by the city and intensely developed with a mix of retail and distribution centers. This new 3-acre (1.2-hectare) site provides 1.5 acres exclusively for Station No. 33, with the balance of the site being master planned for additional county functions, including fire department administration, logistics, and training classrooms. Furthermore, this parcel improved access to two nearby major arterials, improving north/south and east/west response access.

The new site location influenced the design approach and functional arrangement of the station. Contextually, the surrounding neighborhood consists of larger rural residential sites with a majority of these residences providing facilities for horses and livestock. The design phase provided local residents numerous opportunities to offer insight and perspective, resulting in a design that incorporated a number of strategies essential to the proposed design that appropriately responds to its surroundings.

Formally, the solution developed as a series of smaller masses that incorporated forms similar to the surrounding neighborhood, a multicolor palette that helped reinforce the articulation in massing, prioritized orientation of the facility to maintain an enhanced relationship to the street, and which used the existing topography to minimize mass, to minimize the overall height of the facility. This facility successfully incorporates a variety of intentional decisions in order to serve the needs of both the Truckee Meadows FPD and the expectations of the surrounding community.

O'BRIEN
MIDDLE SCHOOL

Reno, Nevada, United States | 2022

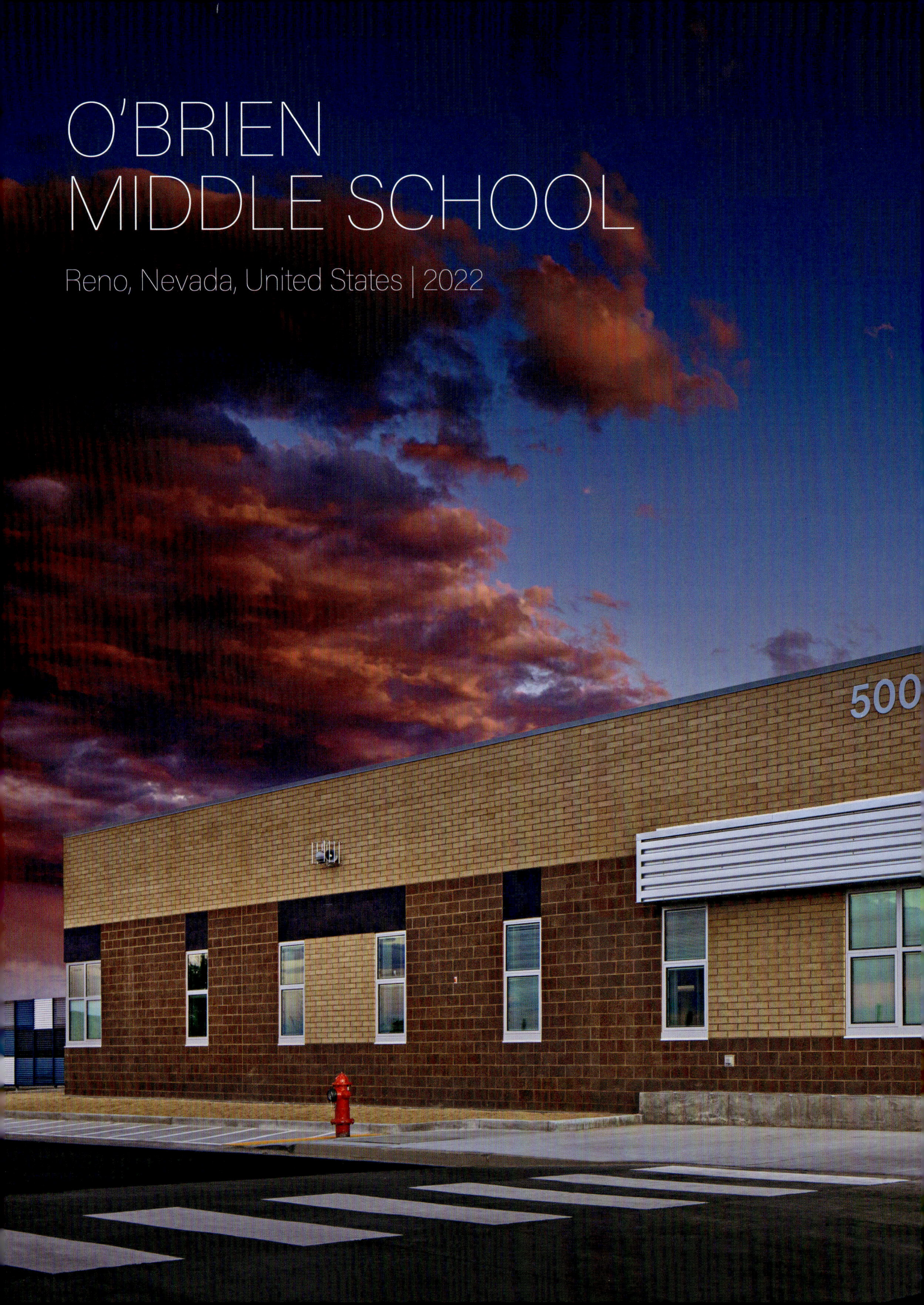

The William O'Brien Middle School is an on-site replacement of the original 1976 facility that provides collaborative education space and increased capacity for 1,400 students. In addition to providing academic space, the new construction improves school campus safety, access, and circulation. Site limitations dictated the development of a new prototype middle school design for Washoe County School District that could be adapted to compact sites. Consisting of five program "building blocks," the design is adaptable to a wide range of site configurations.

The new school is one of the most energy efficient schools in the region. Energy solutions include high-performance glazing, integral user-controlled classroom blinds, and a geothermal environmental system.

Project delivery included an aggressive design and construction schedule. To meet this schedule, construction was broken into three phases: mass grading, building construction, and demolition of existing structure and construction of new athletics fields.

NORTON SCIENCE AND LANGUAGE ACADEMY

San Bernardino, California, United States | 2021

On September 2, 2021, the Norton Science and Language Academy had its Grand Opening to begin a new chapter in the charter school's history.

An innovative, win-win approach to land and program need negotiations with the County resulted in an 18-acre (7.3-hectare) flat vacant lot and $40 million project budget for a brand new 90,000-square-foot (8,361-square-meter) campus. Located in San Bernardino County, California, NSLA is a Dual Immersion Program School that teaches science every day, starting in kindergarten. The school supports underserved students from twenty school districts across Southern California where 90 percent are minority students and almost 80 percent qualify for free or reduced lunch.

At full build-out, the school will serve up to 1,500 students, kindergarten to twelfth grade, making it the first charter school of its kind in the region, with a secondary program that includes courses in Spanish, Mandarin, American Sign Language, and coding. The new campus has seven single-story buildings and a two-story building clustered around three quads with a total of sixty classrooms, library, and administrative offices. There is also an indoor gym, outdoor basketball courts, and playgrounds. An athletics field is planned for the west side of the property. The new campus has a college feel, featuring a multipurpose room and a media center where students can connect directly with NASA missions and science labs.

In concert with the County, the project also includes a 15,500-square-foot (1,440-square-meter) Head Start Program integrated into the campus. This is a one-story, ten-classroom pre-K facility built in support of the County's educational needs for 180 students, and includes administrative offices, warming kitchen, and a parent-instruction multipurpose room.

NORTHEAST CAREER AND TECHNICAL ACADEMY

North Las Vegas, Nevada, United States | 2023

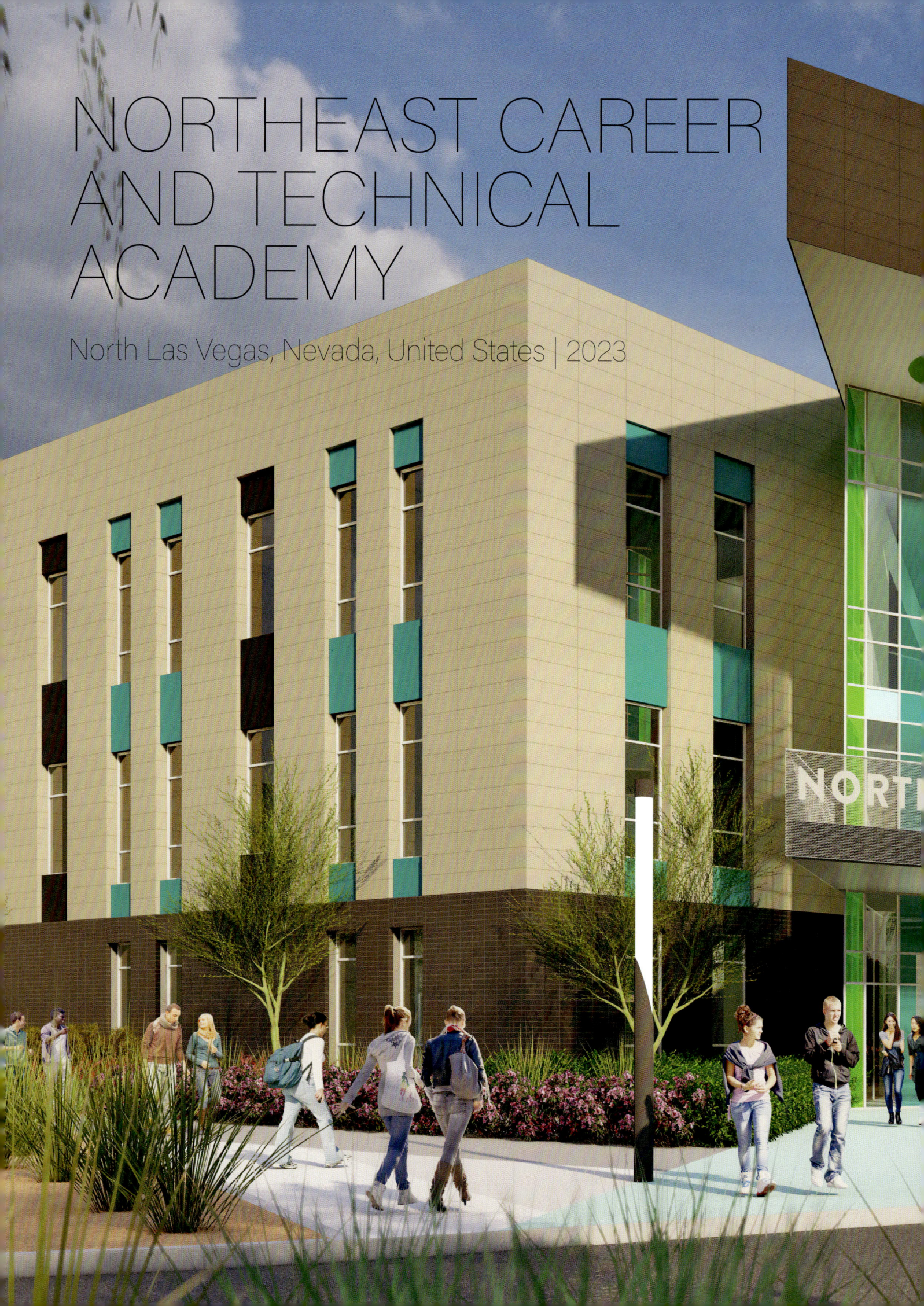

The Northeast Career and Technical Academy, in the Clark County School District, comprises four program-specific buildings arranged to form a protected courtyard with the Commons (Library) as the centerpiece of the campus. This arrangement provides opportunities to connect indoor teaching stations to outdoor learning spaces and extend the flexibility of the classrooms.

The 195,167-square-foot (18,132-square-meter) classroom building houses the majority of the academic programs. To enhance visibility of the academy's programs, and overall collaboration with the general education programs, the Career and Technical Education (CTE) classrooms and labs have been distributed throughout the three-story building, both horizontally and vertically, as have the science labs. Although the programs are distributed, critical functional relationships have been maintained. For instance, CTE programs with high-bay spaces and exterior yards have been grouped together on the ground floor of the classroom building; the health and human services department has been located near the teaching and training department, in order to share kitchen and laundry facilities; and the physics labs are grouped together on the same floor with access to a prep lab. To strengthen the opportunities for collaboration and for flexibility, motorized overhead roll-up doors are proposed to be included in a variety of classrooms and labs, extending both the teaching space into the flexible collaboration zones, which activate the widened circulation spaces and to the exterior (for spaces on the ground floor) to create opportunities for outdoor instructional space. Flexible, reconfigurable furniture will populate the indoor collaboration zones, including mobile white boards, seating, and both standard and high-top tables.

A series of mechanical duct enclosures serve as a visual connection throughout the collaboration spaces on the second and third floors of the classroom building. Large openings are located adjacent to the collaboration zones and are designed to allow daylight to access the core of the building from a clerestory that forms the roof/ceiling of the third floor. The clerestory offers opportunities to integrate operable windows to support nighttime purges through stack ventilation, supporting the district's desire to utilize natural ventilation for a healthier indoor environment. This will be explored further in the next phase. As the centerpiece of the campus, the 10,231-square-foot (950-square-meter) Commons (Library), has been designed for both indoor and outdoor use. In addition to the standard program requirements, a second-floor reading space overlooks the main floor of the Commons. This reading area can be accessed either from inside the building, or from a bridge that connects the classroom building to the courtyard across the Commons. The bridge also provides access to a collaborative outdoor bleacher seating area with an adjacent teaching and projection surface.

We deliberately connected the high-bay gym space with the high-bay student activity center in order to provide opportunities for the 43,465-square-foot (4,038-square-meter) building to support large functions and events, such as cybersecurity red team/blue team competitions and district-wide fairs by opening the spaces to each other. Both spaces visually connect and open to the courtyard, with the gym providing retractable bleacher seating for added flexibility. The 10,975-square-foot (1,020-square-meter) administration building serves as the gateway to the school, providing a single point of entry to the campus after school classes have started. The administration building is adjoined to the classroom building by the kindergarten play yard.

SILVERADO RANCH
DMV SERVICE CENTER

Las Vegas, Nevada, United States | 2025

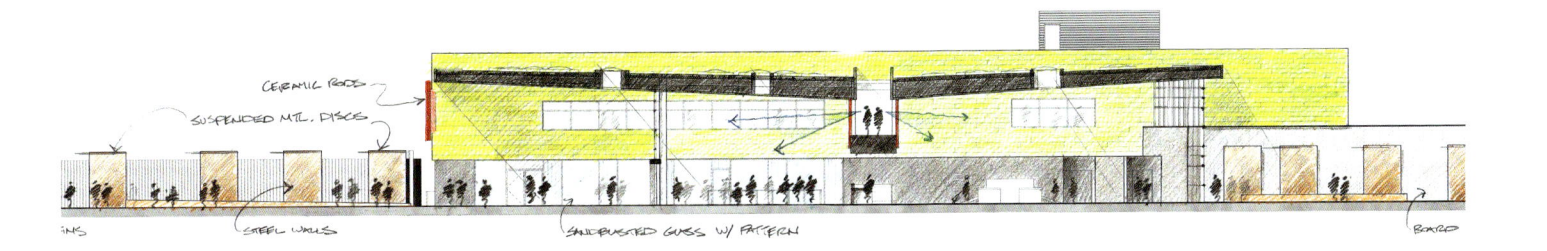

The principal function of the Otay Mesa Land Port of Entry is to facilitate the movement of people and goods between the United States and Mexico. The Otay Mesa Land Port of Entry modernization and expansion project would have presented a grand façade that signified a visual threshold for entry into the United States. Serving as a link between both nations, the new port of entry would provide two public faces: one for international activity between the United States and Mexico, and one for domestic port visitors. This would have generated the need for pedestrian buildings that would serve all international noncommercial interactions and a commercial annex building that would serve all commercial interactions.

During the early phases of design, several topics for exploration and innovation were isolated. Working with border control, our design team proposed five lighting improvements on the port standards that improved lighting quality while saving approximately $60,000 per year.

The region's dry temperate climate requires water conservation. Landscaping that uses regional plants and living machine technology that reclaims all irrigation water on-site would help meet these conservation goals.

The staff occupying the border station would enjoy several environmental innovations. At the truck inspection booths, a remote fresh-air intake would provide a positive pressure, clean air zone. Overhead chilled beams and underfloor radiant heating throughout the buildings would achieve radiant heating and cooling. While effectively reducing on-site energy demands and providing a safer work environment, these environmental innovations would allow the design team to register the building LEED Gold.

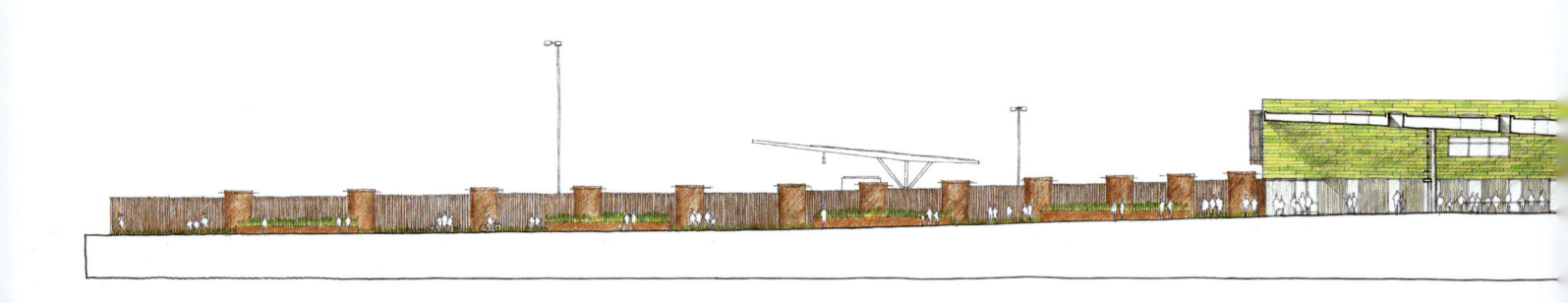

The proposed Nevada Department of Motor Vehicles (DMV) Silverado Ranch Service Center will provide expanded customer capacity to serve growth in the Las Vegas Valley and support advancements in Nevada DMV operations. This new facility will serve as the DMV's Center for Excellence, the training center for new Nevada DMV employees, and incorporates lessons learned from the DMV's previous facilities, including integrating Nevada DMV's digital transformation, clear wayfinding, and providing a welcoming open space to allow for a calm and positive interaction between staff and customers. A first for the State of Nevada, the project is designed to be a net zero energy building, generating as much energy as it consumes.

The new facility will consist of two standalone structures, a new customer service center and a commercial drivers' license facility. The larger of the two structures, the 60,973-square-foot (5,664-square-meter) customer service center, supports the majority of DMV functions and is organized around a large daylit waiting area where all public services are accessed. Given the length of time customers spend at the DMV, the design team developed the waiting area to be "a place one would want to be in," evocative of the grand halls found in early and mid-twentieth century transportation centers. The roof of the waiting area is an expressively modified sawtooth, consisting of a series of undulations that establishes a dynamic spatial interior quality, and on the exterior the undulations are extended to meet the ground, articulating the facility's façade. The articulation of the façade serves two purposes: first, to filter the strong afternoon western light, and second, to dematerialize the west façade allowing entry to the service center.

UNBUILT

OTAY MESA
LAND PORT OF ENTRY

Otay Mesa, California, United States | 2009–2010

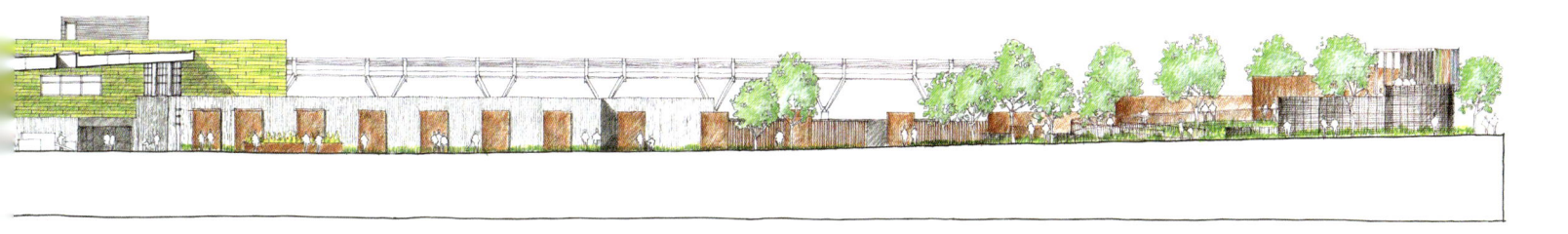

OTAY MESA LAND PORT OF ENTRY

OCT KUNMING HEADQUARTERS

Kunming, Yunnan Province, China | 2019

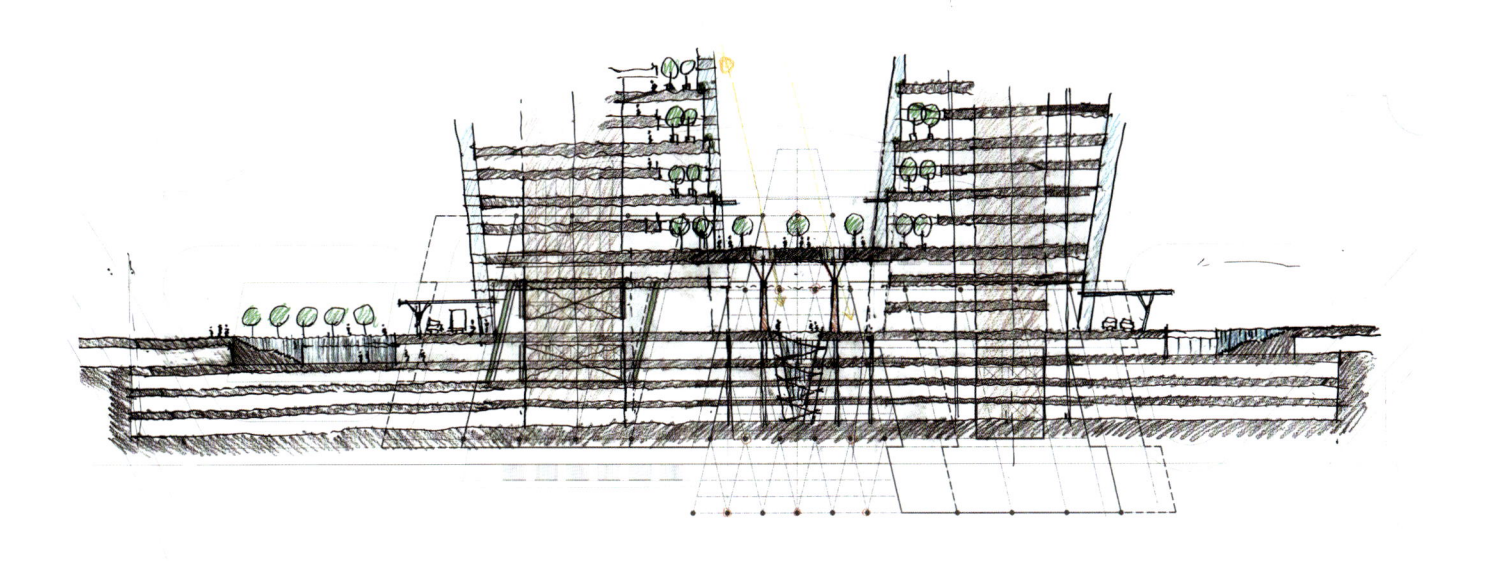

OCT (Overseas Chinese Town) Group Co., Ltd is a large-scale enterprise in China, with leading business sectors in real estate, tourism, urban complex development, theme hotel development, cultural and creative industries, and so on. This project served as a competition entry, submitted to the International Consultation on Concept Design of the OCT Group Headquarters in Kunming.

The OCT Kunming headquarters proposal was for a mixed-use skyscraper—a new landmark, providing a soaring new addition to Kunming rising skyline and displaying the images of OCT Group all around. The intention of the design was not only grounded in its form. It was influenced from the deep thinking of OCT's corporate culture—"Quality Life Creators." The project took inspirations from the local landscape in Yunnan. While lamenting the excitement of Yunnan tourism, from Dianchi Lake to Stone Forest and from terraces to camellias, the design team was also experiencing OCT's philosophy of "relying on nature and being people oriented." The design pushed this ideology with the cooperation of the interior and exterior, both interactively and fluently. These design strategies would have provided a rich experience of nature for people in many ways.

The design was rooted in the functional aspects and put four major programs separately within the twin towers. The towers would be displaced and tilted in order to provide maximum natural sunlight and views. In each tower, sky lobbies were to be added, with an elevated landscape to enrich how one experiences the façade.

At its core, the design was inspired by the experience of people, with landscape elements at the forefront, likening moving through the building to how one moves through nature.

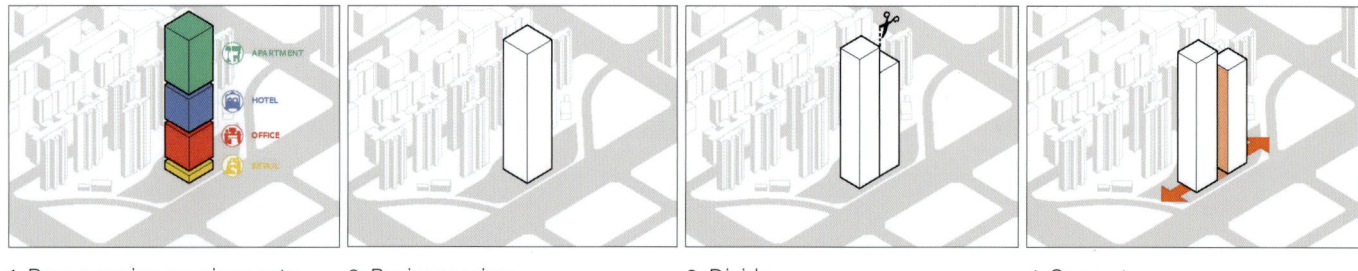

1. Programming requirements 2. Basic massing 3. Divide 4. Separate

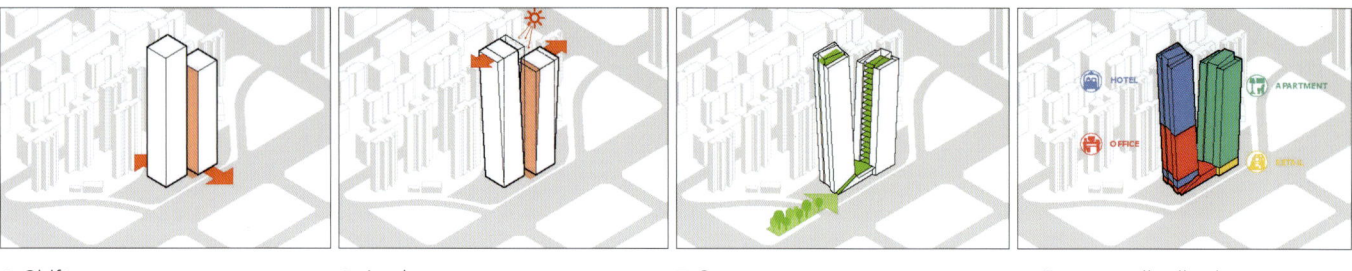

5. Shift 6. Angle 7. Green space 8. Program distribution

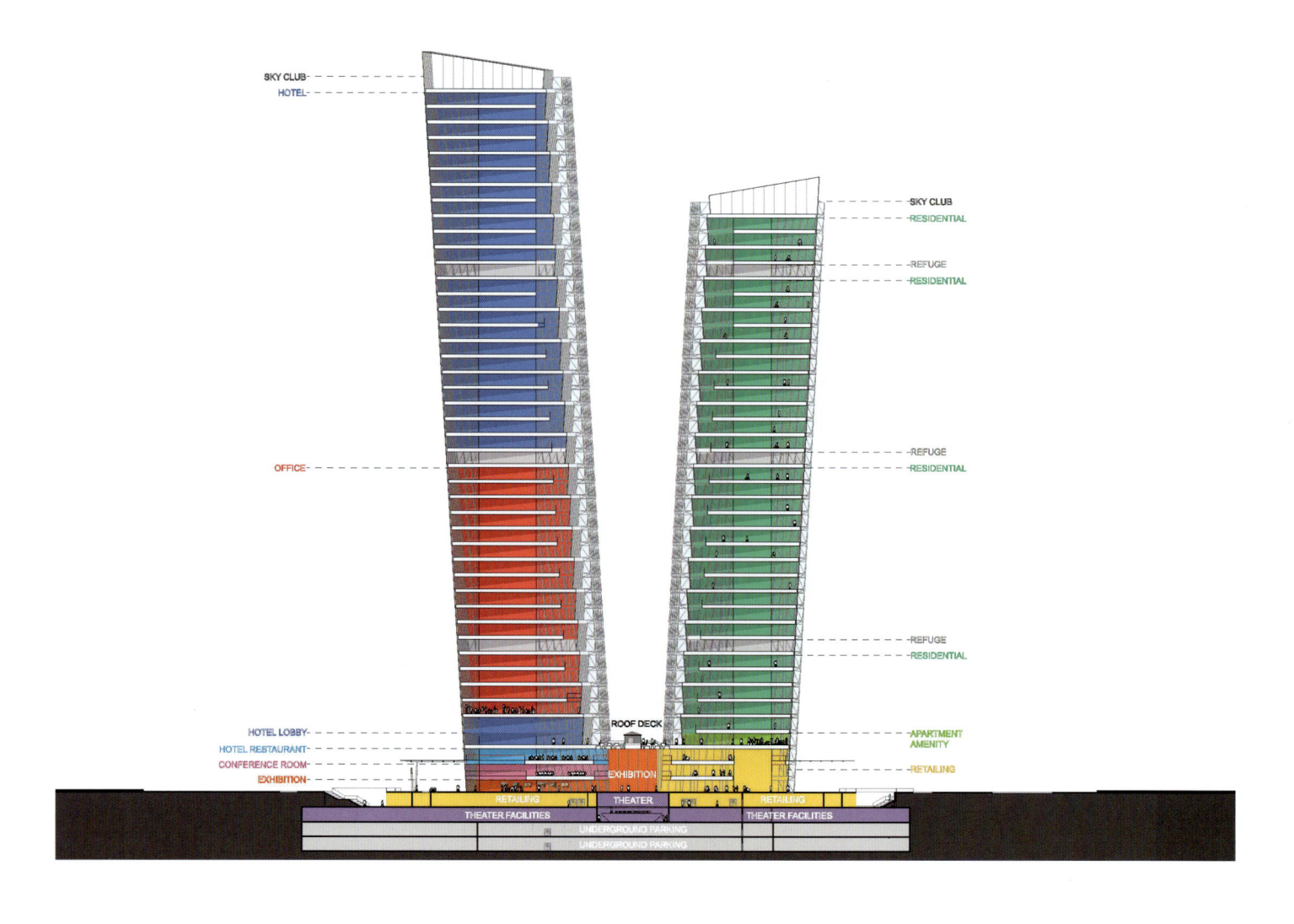

OCT KUNMING HEADQUARTERS

YICHANG
NEW DISTRICT
MASTER PLAN

Yichang, Hubei Province, China | 2013

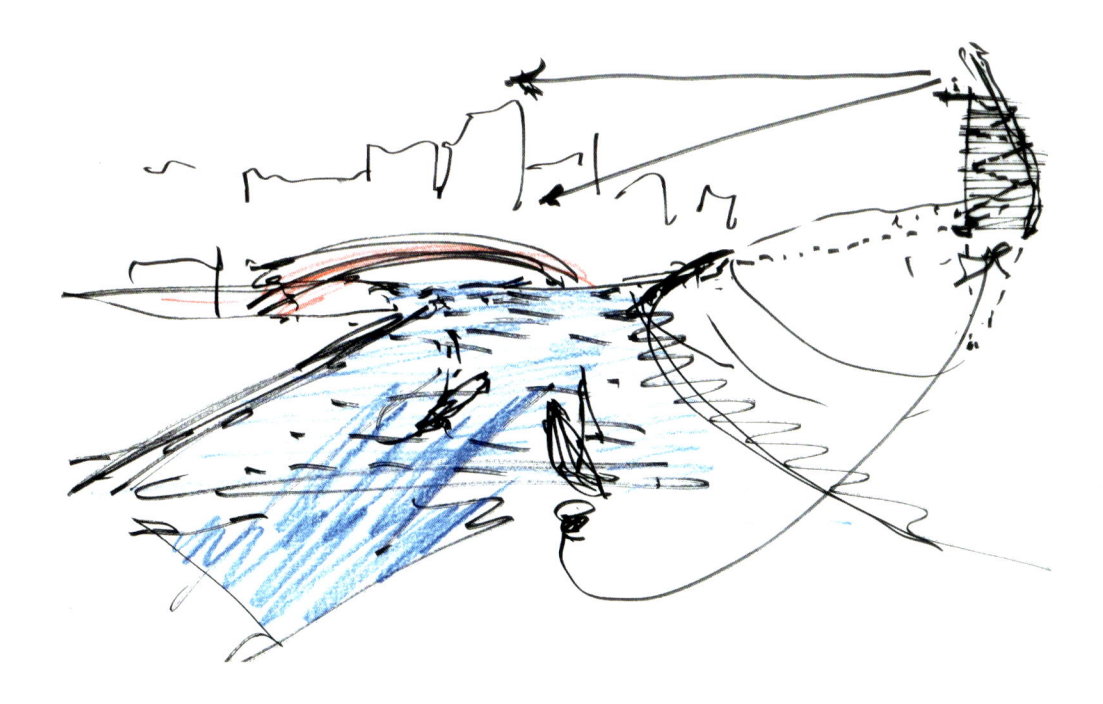

Centrally located in the heart of Yichang Central Park there would be three major cultural buildings: Yichang Museum, Yichang Urban Planning Exhibition Center, and Yichang Art Gallery. The arrangement of the buildings was inspired by the morphological features of the natural landscape of the Three Gorges region, located along the Yangtze River. The buildings were to be compactly arranged in the heart of the site, leaning toward each other and would be connected by a shared platform at the height of 26 feet (8 meters). In this way, the experience of walking on the platform and passing under the buildings would be like journeying along the narrow canyon on the Yangtze River.

The circulation of movement between the buildings would promote a seamless flow for visitors to enjoy the distinct elements of Yichang, such as its rich culture, the arts, and the past and future landscape of the city. The uniqueness of each building would provide an experience for visitors that conveys hometown recognition to the locals and introduces Yichang to tourists.

The planning of three major cultural buildings close to each other was meant to encourage togetherness and elicit a sensation of openness. The platforms of the three major buildings would be equipped with various interfaces such as ramps, stairs, and pedestrian bridges, encouraging fluid movement into the cultural core of Yichang from all parts of the city.

The cultural buildings would surround a shimmering lake; this idea was inspired by a poem about a large lake formed by a dam in the Three Gorges region, which is known to inspire those who visit, and creates feelings of peace and tranquility. The same would be felt at the lake in the cultural district, with its glistening water reflecting the magnificence of the administrative building.

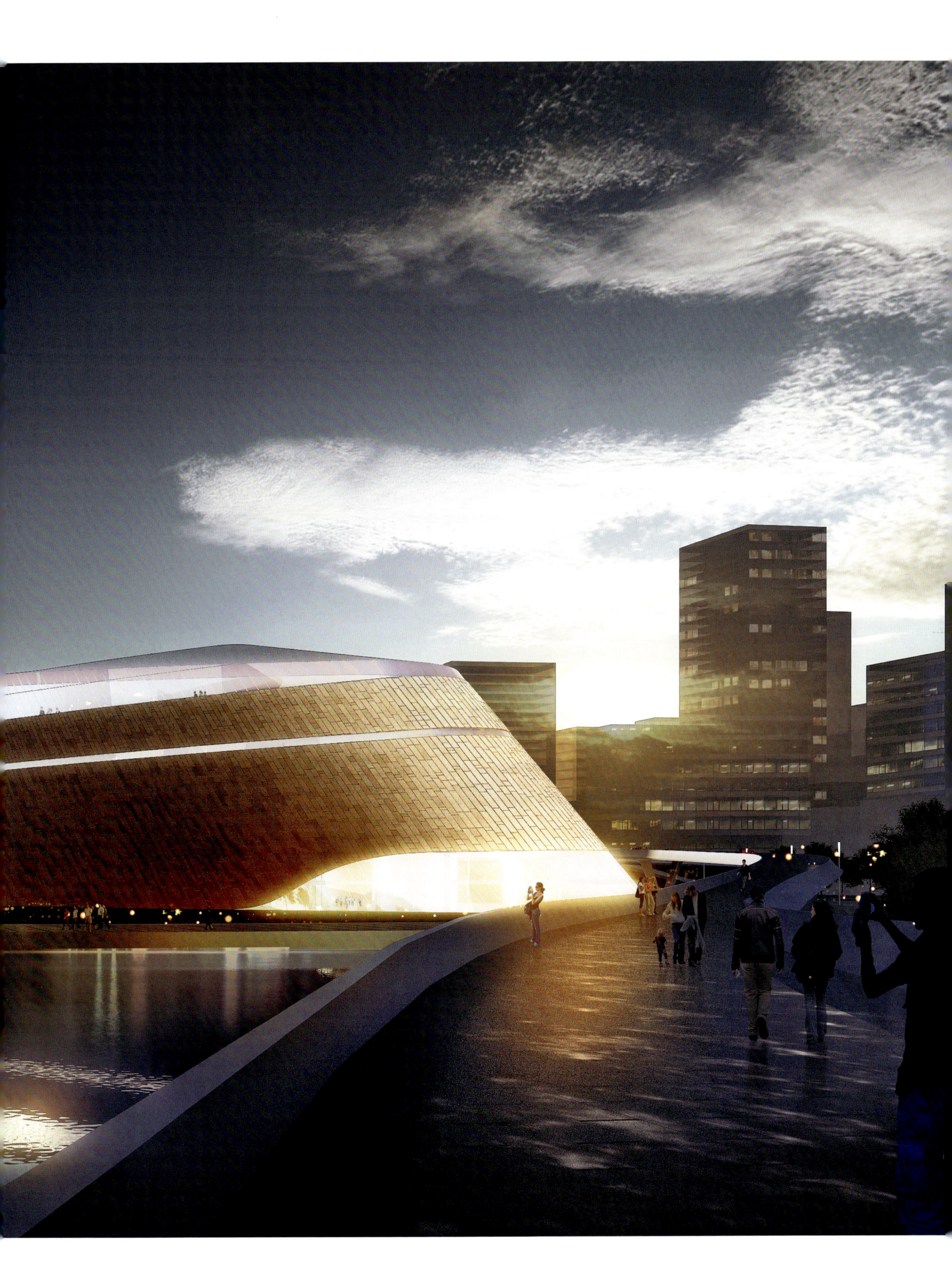

YICHANG NEW DISTRICT MASTER PLAN

CITY OF COLTON NEW CITY SERVICES OFFICES AND SUPPORT BUILDING

Colton, California, United States | 2022

The City of Colton New City Services Offices and Support Building is a master planned expansion of the City's existing 15-acre (6-hectare) community services facility. This environmentally sustainable campus will provide new offices to facilitate the City of Colton's agency services for the public, as well as augment the City's interactive emergency operations center with a new support capacity and planning for a new fire headquarters.

The project consists of 44,539 square feet (4,138 square meters) of new building construction and an additional 20,000 square feet (1,858 square feet) of renovation of existing buildings and structures.

The intention of this project is to establish the new campus as zero-net energy use through the integration of innovative and smart sustainable design standards that result in a target of 60 percent reduction in operational costs while responding positively to the complex environmental conditions prevalent to the region. TSK's design involves harvesting the sun's energy, placing solar power on the existing and new buildings and open-site parking areas, high performance building envelopes, and mitigating toxic stormwater run-off.

All new buildings will take advantage of the regional climate incorporating natural light and ventilation to provide a healthy and energy efficient work environment.

LEGACY

HARRY REID
INTERNATIONAL AIRPORT
SATELLITE D GATES

Las Vegas, Nevada, United States | 2008

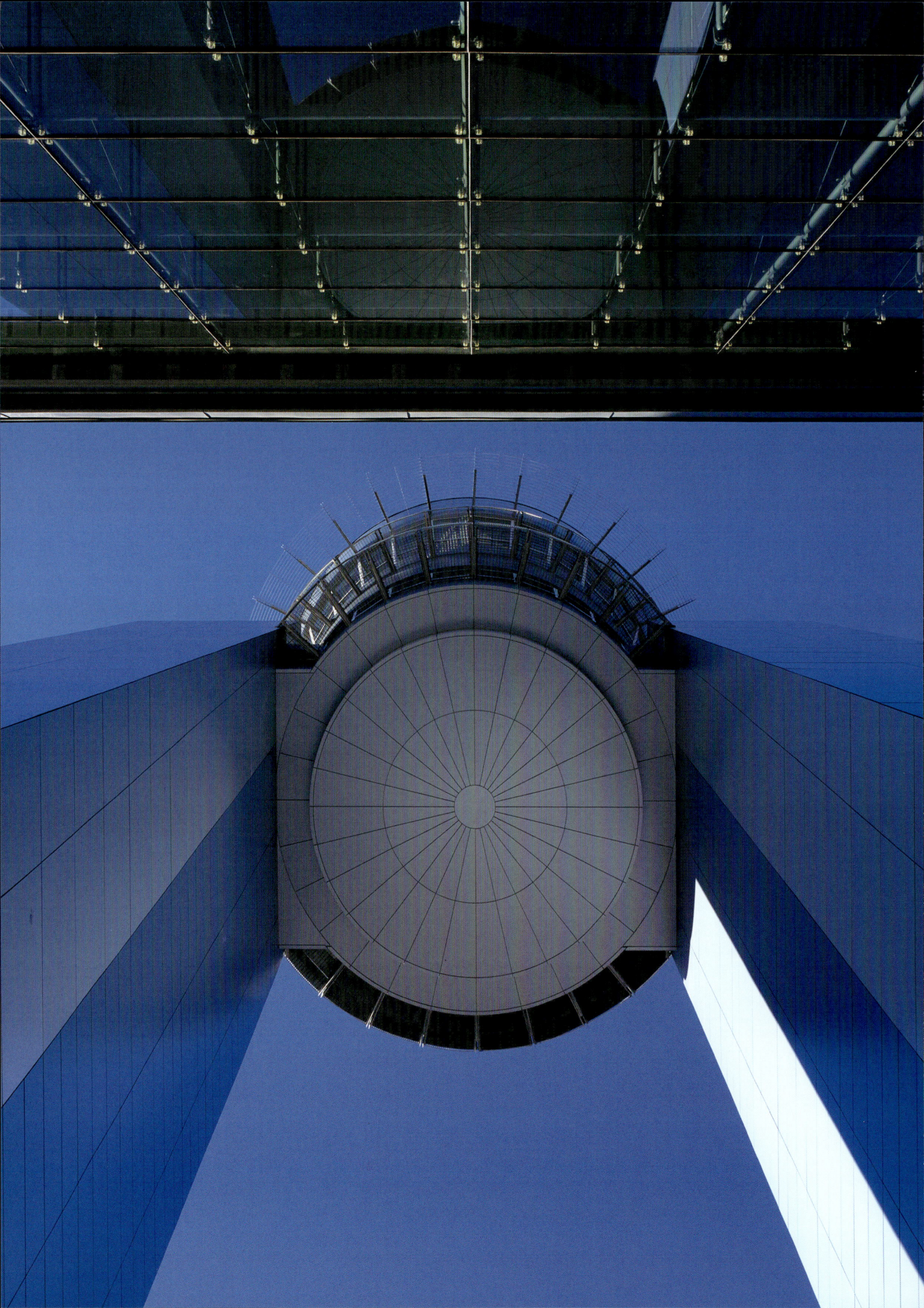

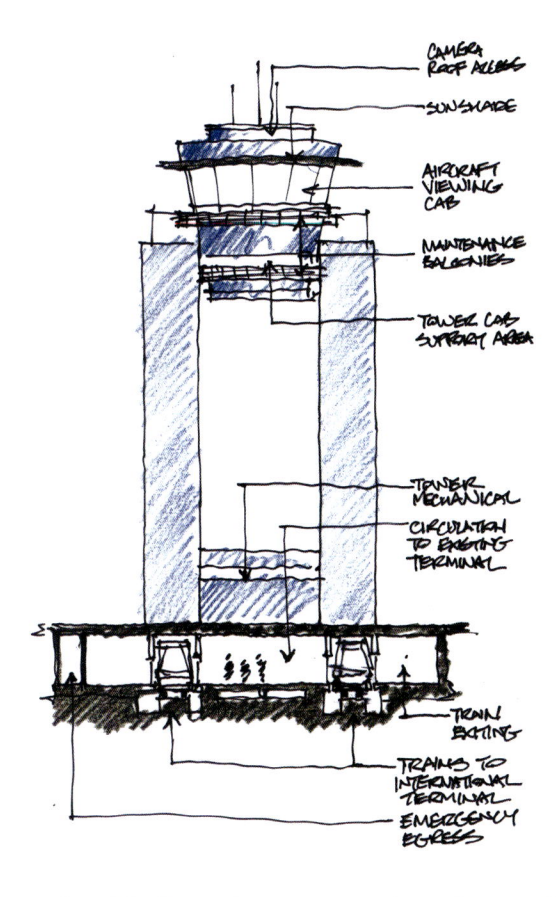

We were the lead designer for this four-phase expansion of one of the nation's busiest tourist airports. Critical issues included celebrating the arrival of the passenger to Las Vegas, establishing visual connections to the city and surrounding landscape, passive wayfinding, and development of back-of-house functions.

This project was an effort to reinstate the passion of passenger travel originally associated with the civic-scaled railroad terminals of the early twentieth century. Major projects such as Grand Central, Penn and Union Stations celebrated the arrival and departure of the rail traveler and at the same time represented a gateway to the metropolis. The Satellite D Gates aspire to that earlier ethos, moving passengers through civic-scaled spaces in a structure that overtly expresses its function as a destination airport terminal.

Passenger terminals must respond to two significant passenger movements: arrival and departure. Passengers arriving in the Satellite D terminal are organized by double-height clerestory center bays, which direct passengers to the central hub of the terminal. Here they encounter a condensed version of the Las Vegas Strip, the "Air Strip," which curves around the central portion of the facility, leading to the Great Hall. The Great Hall bisects the terminal hub, straddling the lower level Rotunda and (in the opposite direction) overlooking the airfield through a large freestanding window wall. The junction between the Great Hall and the escalators leading down to the Rotunda floor features a neon gateway reminiscent of the classic "Welcome to Las Vegas" sign of the 1950s. The floor of the Rotunda features a cast terrazzo recreation of the Las Vegas air map, allowing passengers to recreate their arrival into the city.

As travelers move across this floor to the Airport Transit System (ATS) Station, they can locate their ultimate destination within the valley. Departing passengers, however, experience this sequence of events in a different fashion. Passengers arriving in the ATS Station are presented with tile murals of sixteeen major cities. Each mural design was the product of a local elementary school class and represents the excitement of some distant destination. Crossing the Rotunda to the escalators, the Great Hall ceiling soars overhead with a profile similar to the flight path of an aircraft at takeoff. At the top of the escalator, the rising arc of the Great Hall culminates in a large window that focuses on the point of take-off for departing planes.

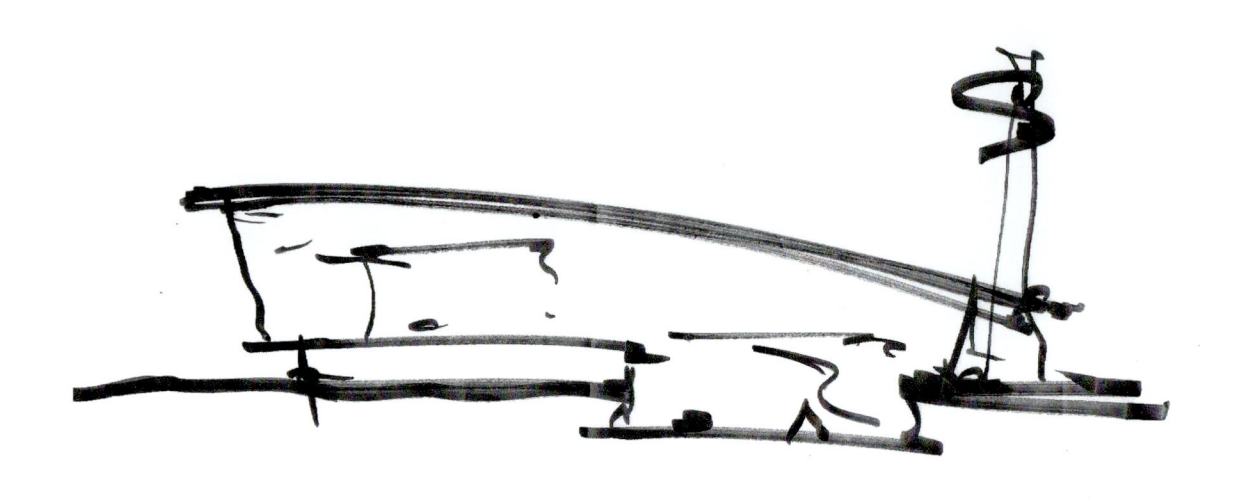

BUILDING SECTION

CLARK COUNTY REGIONAL JUSTICE CENTER

Las Vegas, Nevada, United States | 2005

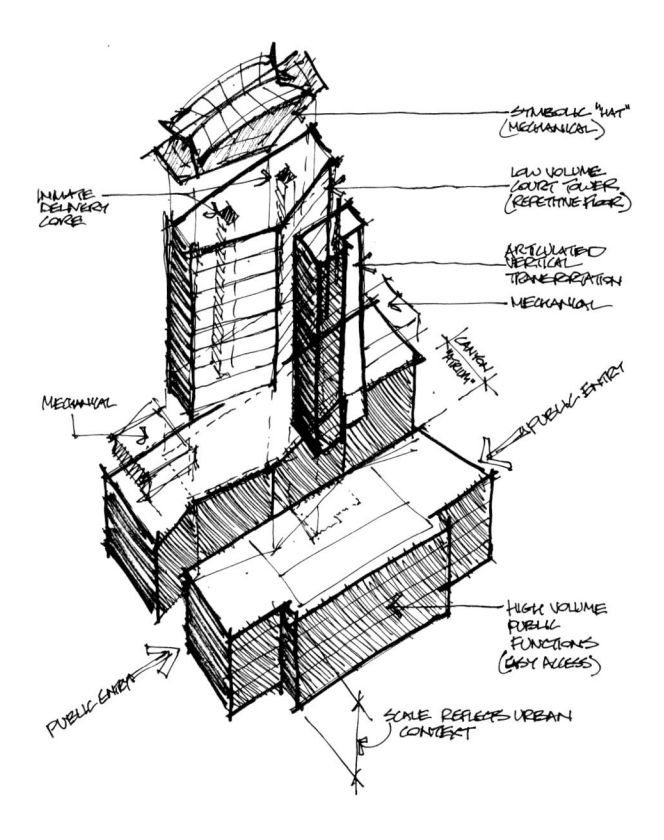

The Clark County Regional Justice Center collocates four court systems within a single facility. The nineteen-story, 710,000-square-foot (65,961-square-meter) complex houses district, justice, municipal, and state supreme courts.

The building echoes the traditional courthouse by providing an elevated glazed entrance plaza (or civic square) that projects a strong identity to the street. A three-story glass atrium draws daylight deep into the heart of the building, a canyon-like area with native sandstone walls inscribed with quotes reflecting the universal concept of justice from various peoples and eras.

The base of the courthouse is designed to accommodate a wide range of public services in a "mall" of justice. The canyon creates an interior street, revealing individual agencies behind storefronts. Public services with the highest-volume demand are located on the entry level.

In keeping with modern courthouse design principles, the regional justice center is served by three circulation systems that separate public, staff, and inmate zones. Security is an integral part of the courthouse design.

To project an open image of the courts to the public, the building was designed to have a positive and welcoming presence, while carefully and discretely integrating state-of-the-art security controls into the building.

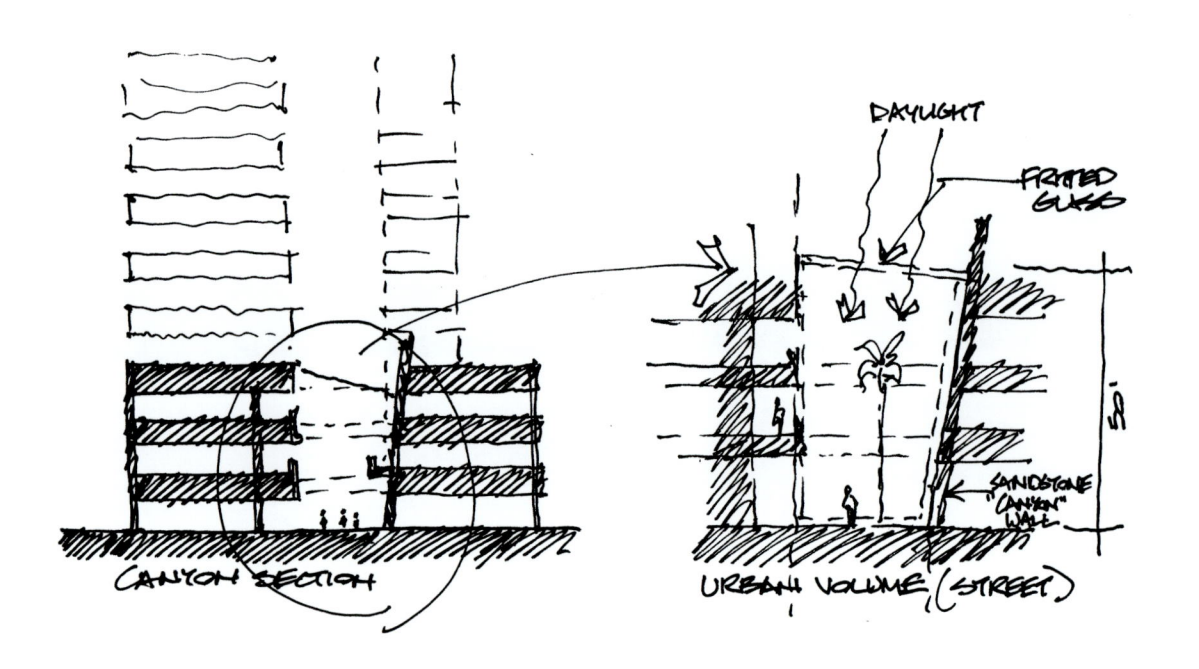

CANYON SECTION

DAYLIGHT

FRITTED GLASS

SANDSTONE "CANYON" WALL

URBAN VOLUME (STREET)

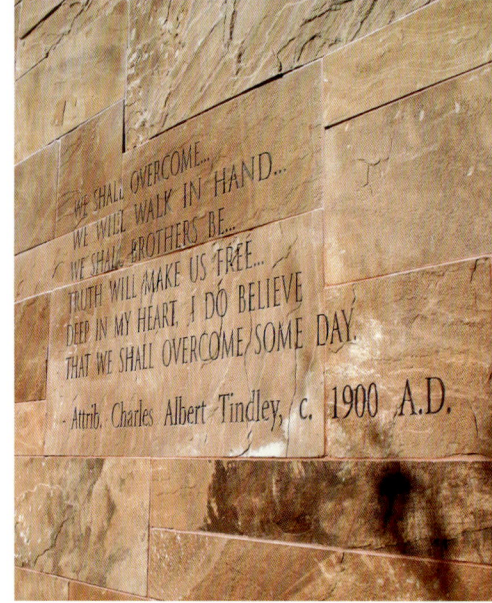

WE SHALL OVERCOME...
WE WILL WALK IN HAND...
WE SHALL BROTHERS BE...
TRUTH WILL MAKE US FREE...
DEEP IN MY HEART, I DO BELIEVE
THAT WE SHALL OVERCOME/SOME DAY.

- Attrib. Charles Albert Tindley, c. 1900 A.D.

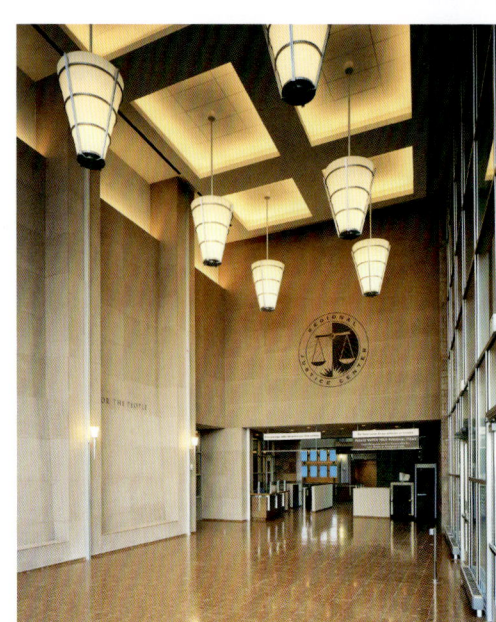

SPRINGS PRESERVE
VISITOR CENTER

Las Vegas, Nevada, United States | 2007

The Las Vegas Springs Preserve is a 180-acre (73-hectare) cultural attraction developed to commemorate Las Vegas's dynamic heritage. It also provides a vision for a sustainable future.

The Ori-Gen Experience is a 53,000-square-foot (4,924-square-meter) exhibit building featuring three galleries and a theater clustered around a rotunda element. The 24,500-square-foot (2,276-square-meter) guest services building houses a gift shop on the first level and a second-level café with a balcony that provides views of the site. We designed these facilities in partnership with Jones Studio.

The Springs Preserve is an interactive environment that highlights the heritage of the springs—a source of water for Native Americans living here thousands of years ago. We organized the project along a creek path—the Ravine Walk—that links the site amenities. The design leads the visitor to engage an immersing desert ravine that the opposing walls of the buildings form. Receded in landscape, the buildings are oriented to afford seek-and-discover experiences that solidify a lasting impression.

The primary challenge was to convey the cultural heritage and story of the site by means of exhibits and interpretive media and other features. We accomplished this by melding buildings and site into a singular expression. Walls blend with the existing and created landforms while commanding a subtle visual presence at the ground plane. These landforms interact with the shaded exterior gathering spaces to create soothing oases. The visitor center received LEED Platinum Certification and features sustainable, regional, durable, recyclable, and low-maintenance materials, including weathered steel, energy efficient glass, recycled composite plastic and wood products, and drought-tolerant landscaping.

Just as the construction materials harmonize with the environment, the basic forms of the buildings seek sensitivity with the land. Long elevations of vertical board-formed concrete walls lead visitors' eyes throughout the site to building entrances and the landscape. Water is one of the project's central themes. The design of the buildings demonstrates how the life-giving resource of water has drawn people together and supported the Las Vegas Valley's culture throughout history. We carefully controlled many of the major experiences around the Springs Preserve by compressing entrances and releasing visitors into surprisingly open and unexpected spaces in order to evoke the flow of water.

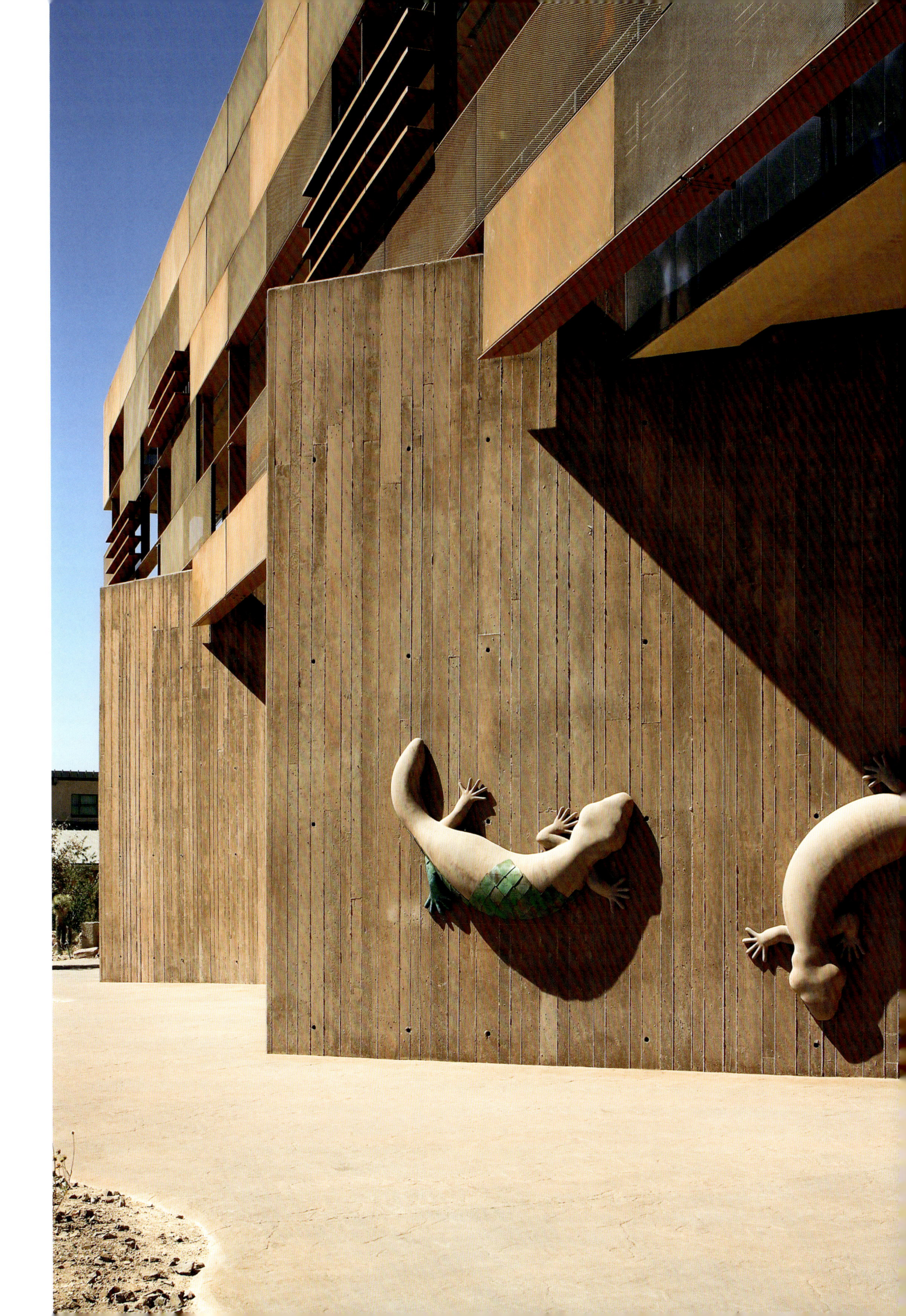

UNLV
STUDENT UNION

Las Vegas, Nevada, United States | 2008

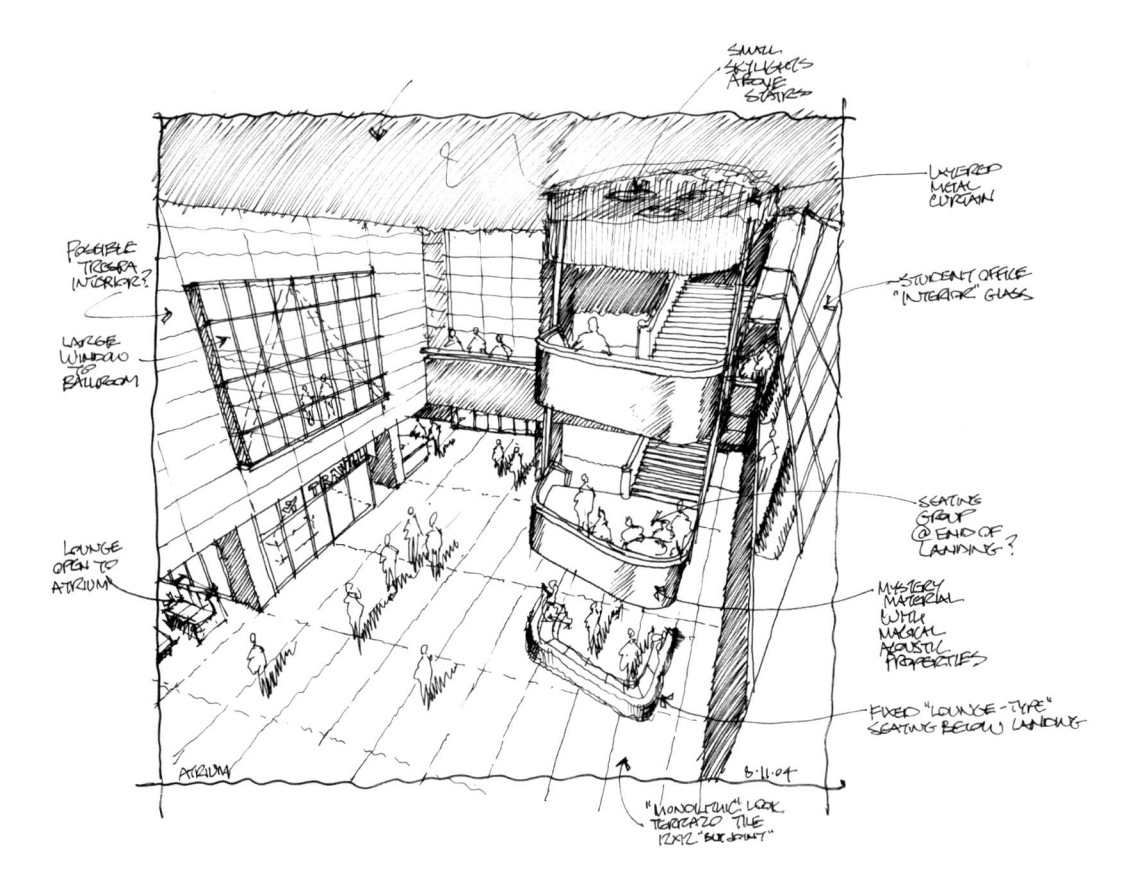

The student union is a focal point for the campus community and an interactive connection to the public in Las Vegas. The building creates an environment where UNLV students can gather informally outside of the classroom, campus organizations can meet, events can be staged, and the public can visit. A major design challenge was to respond to the predominantly commuter-based university population by creating an environment that attracts students to the campus and encourages their involvement in student life at UNLV.

In partnership with Ellerbe Becket, this three-story facility provides spaces for diverse functions and groups. The ground level supports public activity with dining areas, student activities and services, a 300-seat theater, and retail spaces. Semi-public functions, such as a computer lab, computer help center, student lounges, meeting spaces, and a ballroom are located on the second level. Offices for student organizations share the third level.

On the north elevation, a 20-foot-wide (6.1-meter-wide) balcony stretches the length of the building, providing a gathering place overlooking an existing plaza area. To the south, a large courtyard framed by the building is shaded with fabric canopies. This shading structure draws people toward the building, extends the dining space outdoors, and creates a stage for special events. The west half of the courtyard is terraced with 15-inch-high (38-centimeter-high) concrete benches to provide amphitheater-style seating.

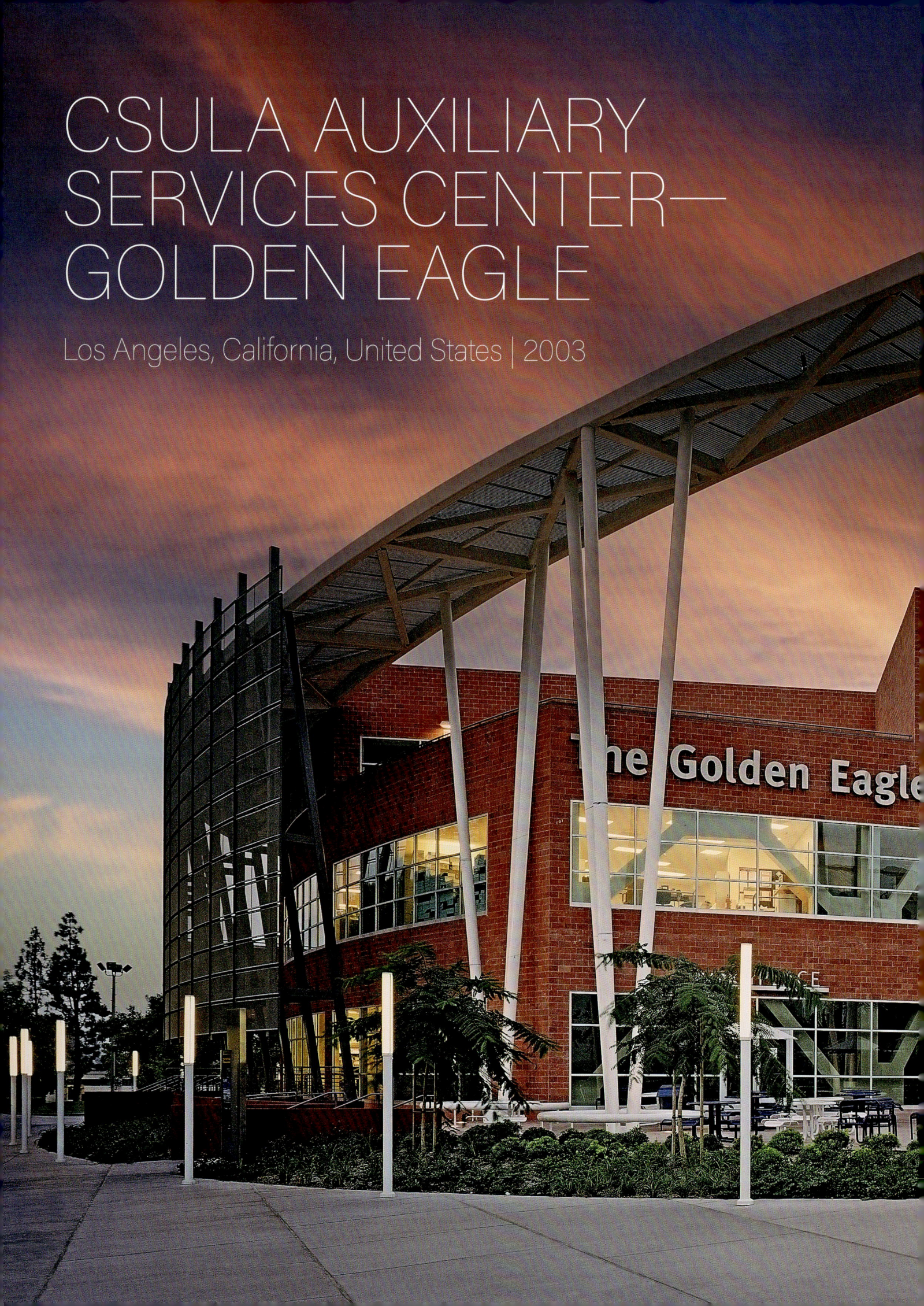

CSULA AUXILIARY SERVICES CENTER— GOLDEN EAGLE

Los Angeles, California, United States | 2003

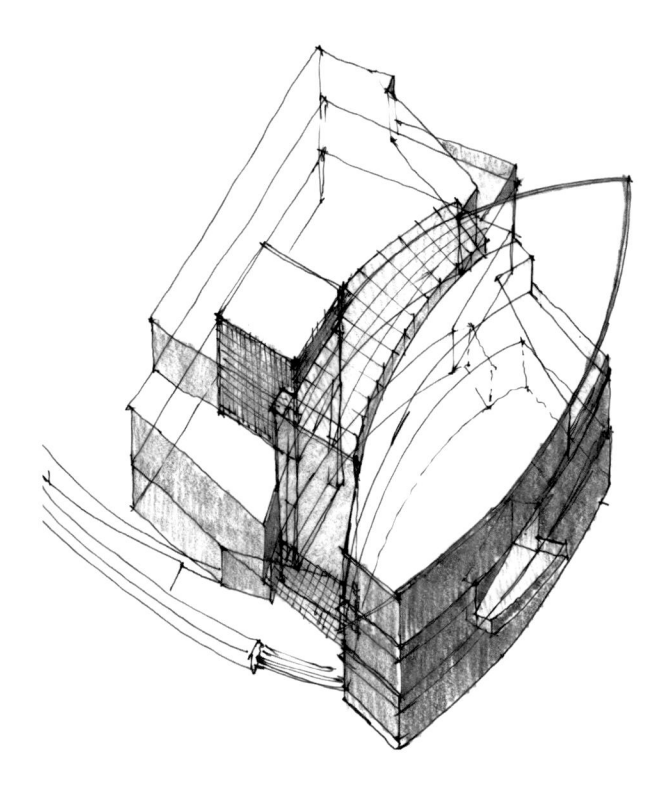

Designed to function as a center for California State University, Los Angeles campus activity, Golden Eagle provides a gathering space for students and faculty. The 103,000-square-foot (9,569-square-meter) building houses a food court, campus store, and university club at ground level. A credit union, classroom space, and additional bookstore area are located on the second level. The third level contains a 600-person conference center and the executive offices of CSULA Auxiliary Services.

The design concept for Golden Eagle separates the facility's food service and retail functions into two distinct operational areas, which are connected above the pedestrian level by a system of sky bridges. These aerial walkways are covered by a lightweight canopy, which provides shade during the day and luminosity in the evening. The curved, arcing edges of the building's east structure are derived from the redirection of pedestrian traffic along the main north–south traffic artery, while the cross axis, delineated by two library buildings, ends in a fully glazed aperture and balcony that faces east.

All conference and instructional spaces on the second and third levels were given close attention to audio-visual and data requirements. Special focus also was paid to mechanical systems and acoustic separation due to the highly disparate and potentially distracting adjacent program elements. Each program element, in effect, was treated as a departmental "zone." This meant providing each zone with its own entry/egress within the overall bifurcated party, individual mechanical rooms, and provisions for differing and adaptable data and audio-visual connections.

HENDERSON NORTH COMMUNITY POLICE STATION

Henderson, Nevada, United States | 2009

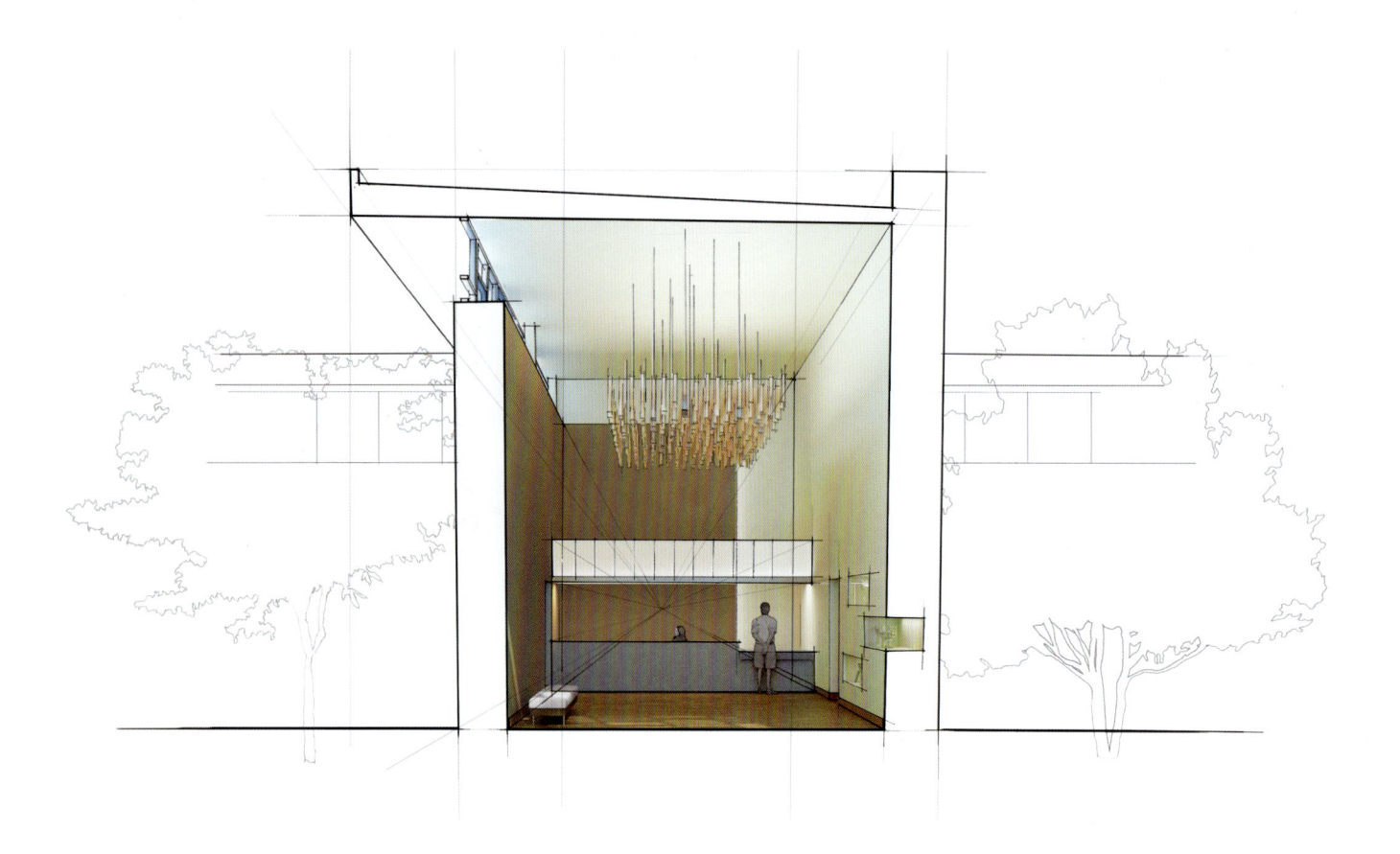

This facility includes training and briefing rooms, offices for the captain, lieutenants, sergeants and detectives, report writing areas for patrol officers, evidence-handling and storage areas, lockers, fitness room, and armory.

To help create a positive presence in the neighborhood, the design for the new police station projects an image of stability and openness. Rectangular massing symbolizes the strength of the department, while warm colors, textured materials, and protective overhangs welcome the public into the facility.

Achieving LEED Gold certification, the new community police station is energy efficient and utilizes alternative energy sources, including a 30kW photovoltaic array installed on top of carports in the employee vehicle parking lot. Clerestory and transom windows with large overhangs and southern orientation bring daylight deep into the building, minimizing the need for electric lighting and maintaining the occupants' connection to the environment around them. Skylights augment the daylighting of interior spaces. The high window arrangement also minimizes exposure for vandals and maintains privacy for the occupants.

MILLS B. LANE
JUSTICE CENTER

Reno, Nevada, United States | 2005

This eight-story complex houses six court rooms and combines all operations of the district attorney's office under one roof. The design effort resulted in a functional, safe, and efficient environment that exceeds current requirements for courthouse security.

The client's primary design objective was to develop a building that conveys to the community a vision of public service, human dignity and permanence, equality in treatment, flexibility, and hope.

The justice center complements and harmonizes with the existing fabric of the downtown cityscape. The building is located on a compact site adjacent to an existing county courts building. In response to this site constraint, we designed a single point of entry that serves both buildings. This shared-use entry has created an identifiable address on Sierra Street that has helped greatly with wayfinding and allowed for the consolidation of security screening functions that resulted in a significant cost savings to Washoe County and City of Reno.

Incorporating artwork into the project was a challenge, as the program did not allow for a formal gallery space. Instead, artwork integrates directly into the building materials. A local artist created a mural on the floor of the main entrance lobby and Washoe County School District students participated in a contest to design a large glass installation located in the landing of the facility's main staircase.

VOLCANO VISTA
HIGH SCHOOL

Albuquerque, New Mexico, United States | 2008

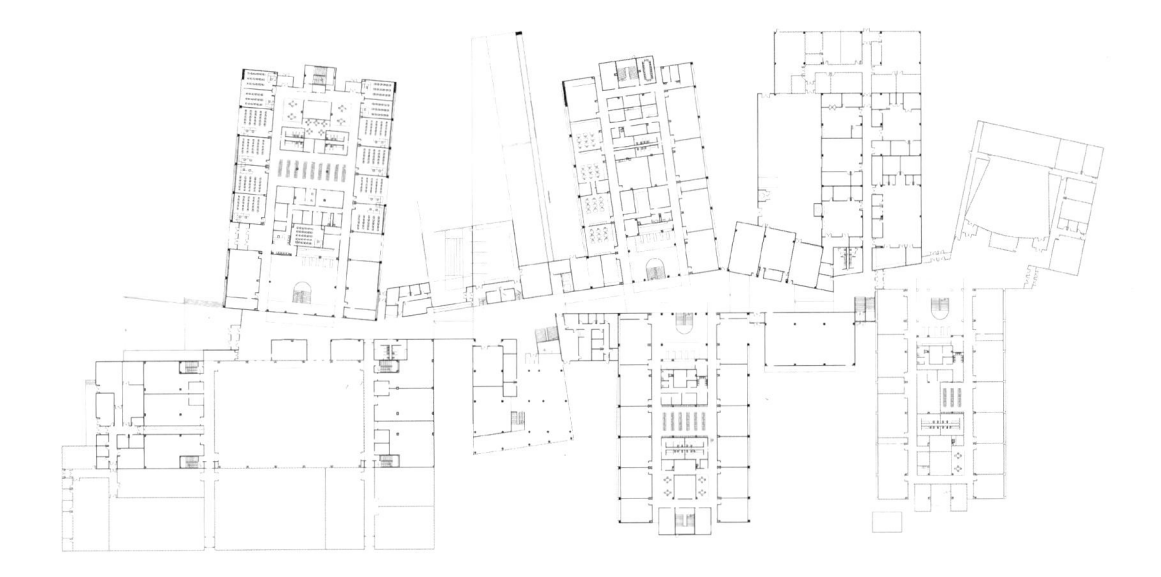

Volcano Vista High School represented the Albuquerque Public School District's desire to improve student learning through facility design and improved teaching practices. Using national and self-generated research, the district wanted to organize the new high school in small learning communities of 125 students to improve student peer support, teacher contact and student socialization. These small learning communities further organize in academies that include five discipline-focused academies and a ninth grade academy. These academies are small separate schools within the larger high school and fully programmed to include administration, lockers, food service and technology classrooms.

The different academies organize around a light filled commons space that serves group activities and food service functions. The building's spine serves to allow interior circulation to shared functions like art and science classrooms, physical education and central administration and parenting offices. The spine also serves to negotiate the site slope over the length of the project campus.

The project site was master planned to function as a comprehensive education center with the district's K-12 facilities. An adjacent segment of the site was further master planned to function as a community recreation center with dual use sharing agreements with the district.

TSK provided design services as a consultant to SMPC Architects.

ARBOR VIEW
HIGH SCHOOL

Las Vegas, Nevada, United States | 2005

In order to keep pace with Southern Nevada's rapid population growth, the Clark County School District site-adapts prototype designs for their new schools. This approach enables the District to meet budget and schedule requirements. Since the completion of the first prototype high schools in 1991, curriculum changes and new standards for daylighting and energy efficiency resulted in a number of design adaptations, all of which were incorporated into this new prototype design.

Located at the main entry, a dramatic interior plaza serves as the hub of student activity for this closed campus. The large multipurpose space at the heart of the school is equipped with wireless web capabilities. This area of the school acts as a thermal buffer between the classroom blocks and helps dampen temperature swings in the adjacent spaces. An innovative mechanical system allows the mall to be treated as a semi-conditioned space, cooled with reclaimed air that would normally be exhausted outdoors from the classrooms. At night, when temperatures fall below 80 degrees, the mechanical system draws in 100 percent fresh air to pre-cool the mall. Thermal mass in the masonry walls and stained concrete floors helps combat temperature increases throughout the day.

To reduce energy costs, classrooms with exterior windows are equipped with daylight sensors to reduce electric lighting when appropriate natural light levels exist. Occupancy sensors in each classroom turn the lights off when a space is not in use, and the entire interior lighting system is automatically turned off when the building alarm is set.

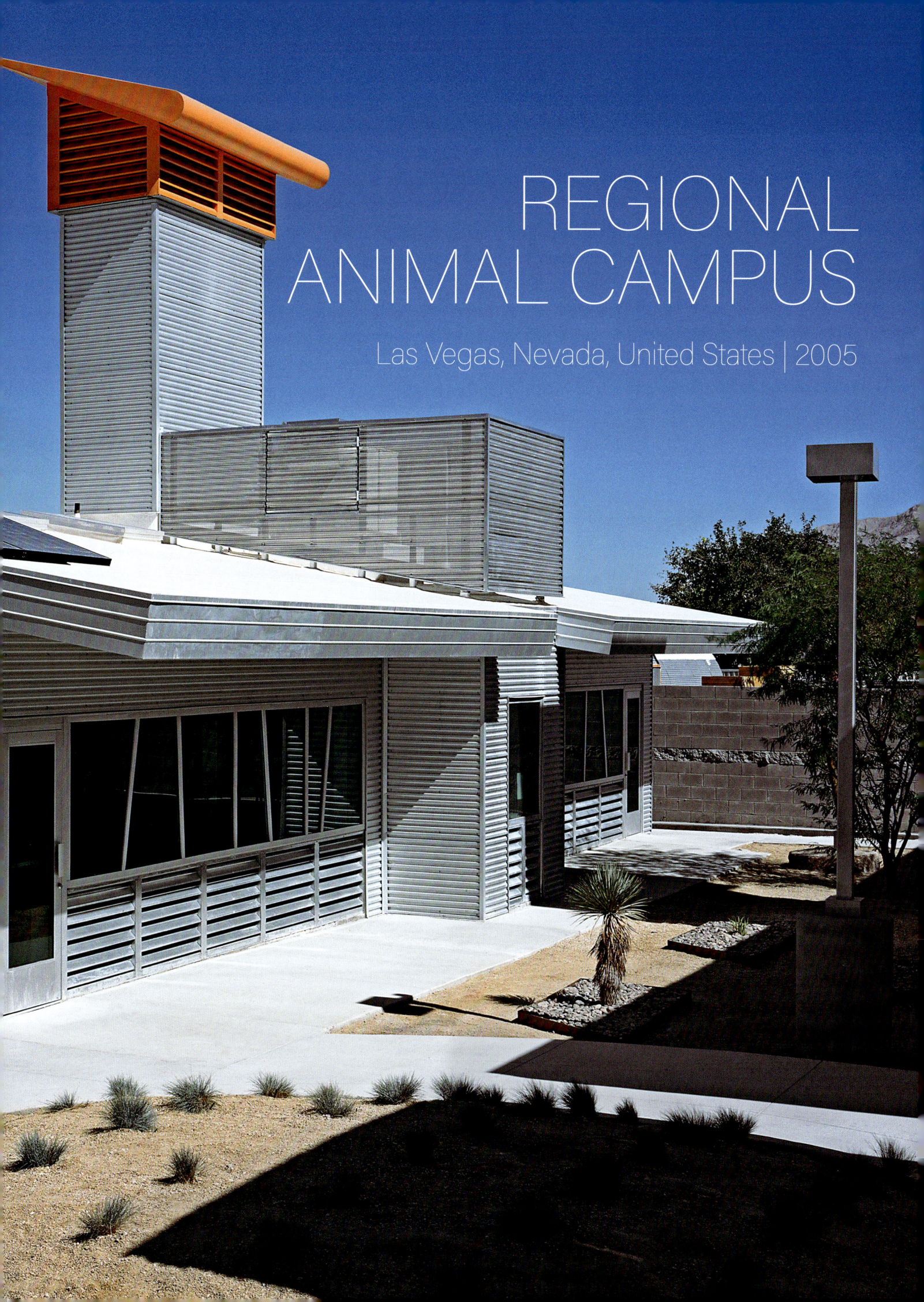

REGIONAL
ANIMAL CAMPUS

Las Vegas, Nevada, United States | 2005

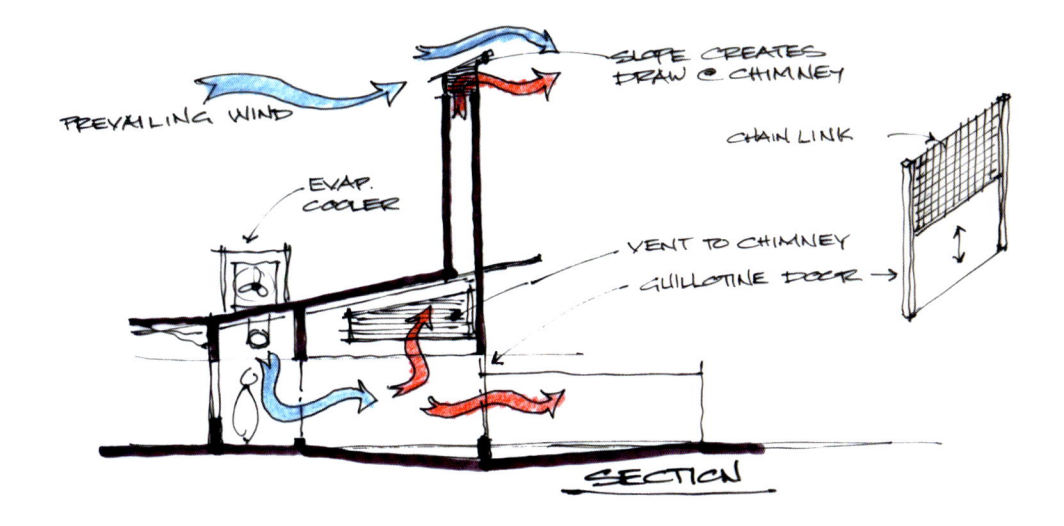

This consolidated animal care campus serves the animal sheltering and adoption needs for the Las Vegas Valley. The project includes expanded adoption facilities for dogs, cats, and large animals, an animal wellness center, and veterinary education center.

The dog-adoption park houses adoptable dogs in groups of ten to twelve within a community of twenty-two bungalows. Beyond fulfilling the basic programmatic requirements, the team set out to accomplish three goals: improve the quality of life for the animals being sheltered; present the animals in an innovative and dignified manner to improve their chances for adoption; and reflect the client's vision of environmental responsibility.

Sustainable strategies cultivate the prevalent environmental resources and utilize them to satisfy over 65 percent of the campus's energy needs. Tall air-exhaust chimneys, which also serve as an iconic symbol for the facility, augments the cooling and ventilation of the bungalows. Large canopies that support photovoltaic cells provide shading in the park between the adoption areas. One of the most salient new technologies employed at the campus is a living machine that treats wastewater for reuse on-site and reduces by 50 percent the amount of water needed to meet the demands of the facility.

This project received LEED Silver certification and it was the first LEED certified building in Las Vegas. The American Institute of Architects honored the campus as one of the country's top ten green projects for 2006. *Newsweek* recognized the development as one of the greenest building projects in the United States.

APPENDIX

AWARDS AND RECOGNITION

Kirk Kerkorian Medical Education Building at UNLV

2023 City of Las Vegas Mayor's Urban Design Award

2021 AIA Nevada Honor Award—Unbuilt Category

North Butte County Courthouse

2017 AIA Academy of Architecture for Justice Award

2015 AIA Nevada Honor Award

2015 AIA Long Beach/South Bay Merit Award

2012 AIA Academy of Architecture for Justice Citation Award

2011 AIA Long Beach/South Bay Unbuilt Award

B-Tech Towers

2021 AIA Nevada Merit Award—Built Category

2-Star Green Building Rating [ASGB Standard]; equivalent to LEED Gold

Las Vegas Convention Center West Hall

2021 AIA Nevada Honor Award—Built Category

2019 AIA Nevada Honor Award—Unbuilt Category

Silverland Middle School

2011 AIA Western Mountain Region Citation Award

2011 AIA Nevada Honor Award

2015 Concrete Masonry Association of California and Nevada (CMACN) - Education Design Honor Award

SouthEND on Water

2023 Henderson's Economic Development & Small Business Awards—Redevelopment Project of the Year

2018 AIA Nevada Citation Award—Built Category

Sahara DMV Service Center

2017 AIA Nevada Citation Award—Built Category

Rex Bell Elementary School Prototype

2017 AIA Nevada Citation Award—Built Category

CXTX Auto City Phase II

2014 AIA Las Vegas Merit Award—Unbuilt Category

US Bureau of Reclamation Date Street Campus

2013 AIA Nevada Merit Award (Building 200)

2012 NAIOP Sustainable Impact Award (Building 1400)

LEED Platinum Certified (Building 1400)

LEED Gold Certified (Building 200)

Truckee Meadows FPD Station No. 33

2021 Concrete Masonry Association of California and Nevada (CMACN)—Profiles in Architecture Award

Otay Mesa Land Port of Entry

2011 AIA Las Vegas Honor Award—Unbuilt Category

2009 GSA High-Performance Green Building Initiative Award

OCT Kunming Headquarters

2019 AIA Nevada Citation Award—Unbuilt Category

Yichang New District Master Plan

2014 AIA Las Vegas Citation Award—Unbuilt Category

Harry Reid International Airport Satellite D Gates

2007 Gold Award for Engineering Excellence

2005 AIA Nevada Merit Award

1998 AIA Western Mountain Region Citation Award

1998 AIA Nevada Honor Award

1998 Southwest Contractor Design Award

1996 AIA Student's Design Detail Award

1995 AIA Nevada Merit Award

Clark County Regional Justice Center

2010 National Association of State Courts Citation Award

2006 AIA Nevada Honor Award

2006 Concrete Masonry Association/AIA California Council Grand Award

2004 International Union of Bricklayers Craft Award

2000 AIA Nevada Citation Award

1999 AIA Las Vegas Merit Award

1999 AIA Committee on Architecture for Justice Citation

Springs Preserve Visitor Center

2008 American Council of Engineering Companies Platinum Award

2008 American Institute of Steel Construction IDEAS Award

2008 Southwest Contractor Award

2007 Newsweek magazine Top Four Designs for a Healthier Planet

2007 AIA Nevada Citation Award

2007 City of Las Vegas Mayor's Urban Design Award

2003 AIA Nevada Honor Unbuilt Project Award

LEED Platinum Certified

UNLV Student Union

2007 AIA Nevada Citation Award

2006 Southwest Contractor Award

CSULA Auxiliary Services Center— Golden Eagle

2003 AIA Nevada Honor Award

2001 AIA Nevada Design Award

2000 Los Angeles Business Council Beautification Award

Henderson North Community Police Station

2010 AIA Nevada Citation Award

LEED Gold Certified

Mills B. Lane Justice Center

2010 National Association of State Courts Citation Award

2006 Southwest Contractor Award

2003 AIA Committee on Architecture for Justice

2003 American Correctional Association Citation Award

Volcano Vista High School

2010 NAIOP Awards of Excellence, Eagle Award, Education Category

2009 Associated General Contractors, Best Building Award for Projects over $20M

2009 Associated General Contractors, Grand Prize for Best of Show

2009 Southwest Contractor, Top Projects of the Southwest

Arbor View High School

2005 AIA Nevada Merit Award

2005 Southwest Contractor Award

2005 International Union of Bricklayers Craft Award

2002 AIA Nevada Citation Award—Unbuilt Category

2002 CEFPI Southwest Region Project of Distinction (Unbuilt)

Regional Animal Campus

2008 Las Vegas Business Press Best Large Green Private Project

2007 *Environmental Design + Construction* magazine Excellence in Design Finalist

2006 AIA National Top Ten Green Building Award

2005 AIA Nevada Honor Award

2005 Southwest Contractor Award

2004 AIA Western Mountain Region Citation Award

2003 AIA Nevada Merit Award

LEED Silver Certified

PROJECT CREDITS

All images are supplied courtesy of TSK, unless otherwise noted.

Kirk Kerkorian Medical Education Building at UNLV

Location: Las Vegas, Nevada, United States

Completion: 2022

Client: Nevada Health and Bioscience Corporation (NHBC)

Consultants: *[interiors and simulation planning]* CO Architects; *[civil]* Poggemeyer Design Group; *[structural]* M.A. Engineering, Inc.; *[MEP]* Harris Consulting Engineers; *[telecommunications, audiovisuals, acoustics, and lighting]* Coherent Design; *[life safety and fire protection]* TERP Consulting; *[building envelope]* Curtainwall Design Consulting (CDC); *[wayfinding and signage]* Hunt Design; *[landscape]* LAGE Design

Area: 125,000 square feet (11,613 square meters)

Photography: Tom Bonner

North Butte County Courthouse

Location: Chico, California, United States

Completion: 2015

Client: Judicial Council of California (formerly California Administrative Office of the Courts)

Consultants: *[civil]* NorthStar; *[structural]* John A. Martin; *[MEP]* IBE Consulting Engineers; *[acoustics]* Newson Brown; *[landscape]* SWA Group

Area: 67,442 square feet (6,266 square meters)

Photography: Bruce Damonte

B-Tech Towers

Location: Shenzhen, Guangdong Province, China

Completion: 2018

Client: Shenzhen Investment

Associate architect: Hong Kong Huayi Design Consultants (Shenzhen) Ltd

Consultants: *[structural, interiors, electrical, and mechanical]* Hong Kong Huayi Design Consultants (Shenzhen) Ltd; *[landscape]* Shenzhen Beilinyuan Landscape Architectural and Planning Design Institute

Area: 3.2 million square feet (297,290 square meters)

Photography: Tianpei Zeng

Las Vegas Convention Center West Hall

Location: Las Vegas, Nevada

Completion: 2021

Client: Las Vegas Visitors and Convention Authority

Associate architects: TVS Nevada Inc., Simpson Coulter Studio, KME Architects, Carpenter Sellers Del Gatto Architects

Consultants: *[civil]* Poggemeyer Design Group; *[structural]* Magnusson Klemencic Associates; Sigma Engineering Solutions, Inc.; *[MEP]* Environmental Systems Design, Inc.; HPA Consulting Engineers; *[landscape]* LAGE Design; *[traffic]* CA Group, Inc.; *[cost estimation]* Rider Levett Bucknall; *[wayfinding and signage]* Hunt Design; *[ADA]* ADA Professional Team, LLC; *[food services]* JEM Associates West, Inc.; *[building envelope]* Heitman & Associates, Inc.; *[life safety]* Howe Engineers, Inc.; *[lighting]* CM Kling & Associates, Inc.

Area: 1.44 million square feet (133,780 square meters)

Photography: Josh Partee

Silverland Middle School

Location: Fernley, Nevada, United States

Completion: 2010

Client: Lyon County School District

Consultants: *[civil and landscape]* Lumos; *[structural]* Tobey Wade; *[electrical]* PK Electrical; *[mechanical]* Technical Designs; *[lighting]* Light + Space; *[cost estimation]* Parametrix, Inc.; *[food services]* DMH Food Service Designers

Area: 94,722 square feet (8,800 square meters)

Photography: Tom Bonner

SouthEND on Water

Location: Henderson, Nevada, United States

Completion: 2016–2022

Client: Blue Skye Development

Consultants: *[civil]* Poggemeyer Design Group; *[structural]* Empire Structural, Inc.; *[electrical]* PDA; *[M/P]* Intrepid Engineering, LLC; Revolution Engineering; *[landscape]* LAGE Design

Area: 14,600 square feet (1,356 square meters)

Photography: Tom Bonner

Sahara DMV Service Center

Location: Las Vegas, Nevada, United States

Completion: 2016

Client: Nevada State Public Work and Nevada Department of Motor Vehicles

Consultants: *[civil]* Atkins North America, Inc; *[structural]* M.A. Engineering, Inc.; *[MEP]* JBA Consulting Engineers; *[cost estimation]* ESG Construction Consultants; *[landscape]* SLA Land Architects

Area: 41,284 square feet (3,835 square meters)

Photography: Tom Bonner

College of Southern Nevada Student Unions

Location: Henderson, Las Vegas, and North Las Vegas, Nevada, United States

Completion: 2019

Client: College of Southern Nevada

Consultants: *[civil]* Taney Engineering; *[structural]* M.A. Engineering, Inc.; *[MEP]* Harris Consulting Engineers; *[cost estimation]* ESG Construction Consultants; *[food services]* DMH Food Service Designers; *[landscape]* LAGE Design

Area: 28,887 square feet (2,684 square meters)

Photography: Jeff Green

Rex Bell Elementary School Prototype

Location: Las Vegas, Nevada, United States

Completion: 2017

Client: Clark County School District

Consultants: *[civil]* Poggemeyer Design Group; *[structural]* Greg Gordon and Associates; *[MEP, telecommunications, audiovisuals, acoustics, security and fire protection]* JBA Consulting Engineers; *[cost estimation]* Calvin Consulting Services; *[food services]* DMH Food Service Designers; *[landscape]* Southwick Landscape Architects

Area: 101,304 square feet (9,411 square meters)

Photography: Tom Bonner

Lincoln Elementary School Prototype

Location: North Las Vegas, Nevada, United States

Completion: 2017

Client: Clark County School District

Consultants: *[civil]* Poggemeyer Design Group; *[structural]* Greg Gordon and Associates; *[telecommunications, audiovisuals, acoustics, security and fire protection]* JBA Consulting Engineers; *[cost estimation]* ESG Construction Consultants; *[food services]* DMH Food Service Designers; *[landscape]* Southwick Landscape Architects

Area: 105,922 square feet (9,840 square meters)

Photography: Tom Bonner

CXTX Auto City Phase II

Location: Kunming, Yunnan Province, China

Completion: 2021

Client: Runsun Development Group

Associate architect: YIC Architectural

Consultants: *[structural, MEP, interiors, and landscape]* YIC Architectural

Area: 3.7 million square feet (343,741 square meters)

Photography: Yilong Zhao

Topaz

Location: Los Angeles, California, United States

Completion: 2018

Client: JADE Enterprises, LLC

Consultants: *[civil]* Nick Kazem, Inc.; *[structural]* Englekirk Structural Engineers; *[mechanical]* SPEC Group, Inc.; *[electrical]* Accessible Consulting Engineers; *[interiors]* Style Interior Design, Inc.; *[fire protection]* AZTEC Fire Protection, Inc.; *[landcape]* Hongjoo Kim Landscape Architects

Area: 282,200 square feet (26,217 square meters)

Clark County Fire Station No. 61

Location: Las Vegas, Nevada, United States

Completion: 2021

Client: Clark County

Consultants: *[civil]* Poggemeyer Design Group; *[structural]* M.A. Engineering, Inc.; *[MEP]* Intrepid Engineering; *[cost estimation]* OCMI; *[landscape]* LAGE Design

Area: 10,311 square feet (958 square meters)

Photography: Michael Tessler

U.S. Bureau of Reclamation Date Street Campus

Location. Boulder City, Nevada, United States

Completion: 2011 & 2013

Client: Bureau of Reclamation

Consultants: *[civil]* Lochsa Engineering; *[structural]* LERA Consulting Structural Engineers (Building 1400), Greg Gordon and Associates (Buildings 100, 200); *[historic]* Mel Green and Associates; *[acoustics and MEP]* NV5 (Building 200); *[landscape]* Quercus

Area: *[Building 1400]* 49,000 square feet (4,552 square meters); *[Building 200]* 15,300 square feet (1,421 square meters); *[Building 100]* 10,800 square feet (1,003 square meters)

Photography: Tom Bonner (Building 1400), Jeff Green (Buildings 100, 200)

Sherman Oaks Center for Enriched Studies

Location: Los Angeles, California, United States

Completion: 2022

Client: Los Angeles Unified School District

Consultants: *[civil and structural]* Brandow & Johnston, Inc.; *[design build contractor]* Sinanian Development, Inc.; *[historic]* Historic Resources Group; *[geotechnical]* Gorian Engineering; *[MEP]* P2S Engineering; *[acoustics]* Waveguide, LLC; *[landscape]* EPT Design

Area: 101,304 square feet (9,411 square meters)

John F. Miller School

Location: Las Vegas, Nevada, United States

Completion: 2013

Client: Clark County School District

Consultants: *[civil]* Poggemeyer Design Group; *[structural]* Greg Gordon and Associates; *[MEP]* NV5; *[food services]* DMH Food Service Designers; *[landscape]* Southwick Landscape Architects

Area: 68,875 square feet (6,399 square meters)

Photography: Tom Bonner

Truckee Meadows FPD Station No. 33

Location: Reno, Nevada, United States

Completion: 2018

Client: Washoe County

Consultants: *[civil]* CFA; *[structural]* Forbes-Linchpin; *[electrical]* Jensen; *[mechanical and plumbing]* CR Engineering; *[cost estimation]* OCMI; *[landscape]* GreenDesign

Area: 10,662 square feet (991 square meters)

Photography: Vance Fox

O'Brien Middle School

Location: Reno, Nevada, United States

Completion: 2022

Client: Washoe County School District

Consultants: *[civil]* Resource Concepts, Inc.; *[structural]* Nelson Wilcox Structural Engineers; *[mechanical]* Ainsworth Associates; *[electrical]* Dinter Engineering; *[food services]* DMH Food Service Designers; *[landscape]* Design Workshop

Area: 178,500 square feet (16,583 square meters)

Photography: Tom Bonner

Norton Science & Language Academy

Location: San Bernardino, California, United States

Completion: 2021

Client: Lewis Center for Educational Research

Consultants: *[civil]* Kimley Horn & Associates; *[structural]* KPFF; *[MEP]* IMEG Corporation; *[landscape]* Hongjoo Kim Landscape Architects

Area: 90,000 square feet (8,361 square meters)

Photography: Tom Bonner

Northeast Career Technical Academy

Location: North Las Vegas, Nevada, United States

Completion: 2023

Client: Clark County School District

Consultants: *[civil]* Poggemeyer Design Group; *[structural]* M.A. Engineering, Inc.; *[MEP]* TJK Consulting Engineers; *[life safety and fire protection]* TERP

Consulting; *[acoustics]* Auralworth Acoustics; *[cost estimation]* OCMI; *[food services]* DMH Food Service Designers; *[landscape]* LAGE Design

Area: 259,838 square feet (24,140 square meters)

Silverado Ranch DMV Service Center

Location: Las Vegas, Nevada, United States

Estimated completion: 2025

Client: Nevada State Public Work and Nevada Department of Motor Vehicles

Consultants: *[civil]* Poggemeyer Design Group; *[structural]* M.A. Engineering, Inc.; *[MEP]* Harris Consulting Engineers; *[fire protection]* TERP Consulting; *[acoustics]* Auralworth Acoustics; *[cost estimation]* OCMI; *[landscape]* SLA Land Architects

Area: 60,973 square feet (5,664 square meters)

Otay Mesa Land Port of Entry

Location: Otay Mesa, California, United States

Design: 2009–2010

Client: US General Services Administration

Consultants: *[civil]* Atkins; WH Pacific; Malpass Design Group; *[structural]* Greg Gordon and Associates; *[MEP]* WH Pacific; IBE Consulting Engineers; *[interiors]* Ronnette Riley Architect; *[geotechnical]* Moore Twining; *[cost estimation]* Balis & Company; *[landscape]* Charles Anderson + Design Workshop

Area: 428,300 square feet (39,790 square meters) over 51 acres (20.6 hectares)

OCT Kunming Headquarters

Location: Kunming, Yunnan Province, China

Design: 2019

Client: OCT (Overseas Chinese Town) Group Co., Ltd

Area: 1,032,259 square feet (95,900 square meters)

Yichang New District Master Plan

Location: Yichang, Hubei Province, China

Design: 2013

Client: Yichang Urban Planning Bureau

Area: 2.5 million square feet (232,258 square meters)

City of Colton New City Services Offices and Support Building

Location: Colton, California, United States

Completion: 2022

Client: City of Colton

Area: 60,539 square feet (5,996 square meters)

Harry Reid International Airport Satellite D Gates

Location: Las Vegas, Nevada, United States

Completion: 2008

Client: Clark County Department of Aviation

Associate architect: Leo A Daly

Consultants: *[structural and MEP]* Leo A Daly; *[graphics and signage]* Wayne Hunt Design; *[interiors]* Fielden & Partners; *[lighting]* LAM Partners; *[fire analysis and ADA]* Rolf Jensen & Associates; *[soils]* Terracon

Area: 1.1 million square feet (102,193 square meters)

Photography: Alan Karchmer

Clark County Regional Justice Center

Location: Las Vegas, Nevada, United States

Completion: 2005

Client: Clark County

Consultants: *[civil]* Poggemeyer Design Group; *[structural]* Bennett & Jimenez, Inc.; Leslie E. Robertson Associates; *[construction]* ESG Construction Consultants; *[MEP]* JBA Consulting Engineers; *[programming]* Dan Wiley; *[lighting]* Rolf Jensen & Associates; LAM Partners; *[court design]* HDR; *[vertical transportation]* Lerch Bates; *[acoustics and audiovisuals]* Paoletti & Associates, Inc.; *[signage]* Hunt Design; *[telecommunications]* KAI Consulting; Robert Director Telecommunications; *[security design]* Buford Goff & Associates; Robert Glass & Associates, Inc.; *[value engineer]* Parametrix, Inc.; *[landscape]* SWA Group

Area: 710,000 square feet (65,961 square meters)

Photography: Alan Karchmer

Springs Preserve Visitor Center

Location: Las Vegas, Nevada, United States

Completion: 2007

Client: Las Vegas Valley Water District

Consultants: *[civil]* Poggemeyer Design Group; *[structural]* LERA Consulting Structural Engineers; *[MEP]* NV5; *[acoustics]* Arup; *[lighting]* LAM Partners; *[exhibit design]* West Office; *[landscape]* E Group

Area: 77,500 square feet (7,200 square meters)

Photography: Tom Bonner

UNLV Student Union

Location: Las Vegas, Nevada, United States

Completion: 2008

Consultants: *[civil]* Lochsa Engineering; *[structural, interiors, and MEP]* Ellerbe Becket; *[acoustics]* Martin Newson; *[lighting]* DNA; *[wayfinding]* Hunt Design; *[food services]* DMH Food Service Designers; *[landscape]* SWA Group

Area: 135,000 square feet (12,542 square meters)

Photography: Tom Bonner

CSULA Auxiliary Services Center—Golden Eagle

Location: Los Angeles, California, United States

Completion: 2003

Client: California State University, Los Angeles

Architect of record: WOU & Partners

Consultants: *[civil]* ASL; Tetra Tech; *[MEP and structural]* Arup; *[wayfinding]* Hunt Design

Area: 103,000 square feet (9,569 square meters)

Photography: Tom Bonner

Volcano Vista High School

Location: Albuquerque, New Mexico, United States

Completion: 2008

Client: Albuquerque Public School District

Architect of record: SMPC Architects

Consultants: *[civil]* Bohannan Huston Inc.; *[structural]* Chavez—Grieves Consulting Engineers; *[mechanical and plumbing]* Harmeyer Nellos Engineering; *[electrical]* A C Engineering (THE Group); *[acoustics]* Robert Jones; *[theater]* D.L. Adams; *[landscape]* MRWM

Area: 486,206 square feet (45,170 square meters)

Photography: Charles McGrath

Henderson North Community Police Station

Location: Henderson, Nevada, United States

Completion: 2009

Client: City of Henderson

Consultants: *[civil]* Malpass Design Group; *[structural]* Greg Gordon and Associates; *[MEP]* Harris Consulting Enginners; *[landscape]* Southwick Landscape Architects

Area: 35,600 square feet (3,307 square meters)

Photography: Terry Mahanna

Mills B. Lane Justice Center

Location: Reno, Nevada, United States

Completion: 2005

Client: Washoe County

Consultants: *[civil and landscape]* CFA; *[structural]* Martin & Peltyn; *[MEP]* NV5; *[programming]* Dan Wiley; *[wayfinding]* Hunt Design

Area: 150,000 square feet (13,935 square meters)

Photography: Tom Bonner

Arbor View High School

Location: Las Vegas, Nevada, United States

Completion: 2005

Client: Clark County School District

Consultants: *[structural]* GFG Engineering Consultants; *[MEP]* JBA Consulting Engineers

Area: 330,452 square feet (30,700 square meters)

Photography: Alan Karchmer

Regional Animal Campus

Location: Las Vegas, Nevada, United States

Completion: 2005

Client: The Animal Foundation

Consultants: *[civil]* Lochsa Engineering; *[structural]* American Structural Engineers; *[mechanical and electrical]* Harris Consulting Engineers; *[sustainability]* Battle-McCarthy; *[geotechnical]* Terracon; *[landscape]* WRG Design, Inc.

Area: 14,000 square feet (1,300 square meters)

Photography: Tom Bonner

THANK YOU

TSK would like to thank our clients around the world who made this work possible. It is working on your projects throughout the years that has shaped who we are as designers and practitioners. Our architecture comes from great clients who trust us to bring their visions to fruition. It is a process of hard work, exploration, and collaboration to make the buildings we do. It has been our privilege to work with all of you since our inception in 1960.

We have been fortunate to work with some of the finest consultants and contractors in the world. These projects are a testament to their talent and dedication to making quality buildings.

The real magic behind what we do is our amazing staff, both past and present. Without their knowledge, experience, and passionate enthusiasm we could not have designed these beautiful projects. The consistent effort of these people over six decades is a testament to great leadership. TSK is particularly grateful for the vision of George Tate and Bill Snyder who founded the firm all those years ago.

Published in Australia in 2023 by
The Images Publishing Group Pty Ltd
ABN 89 059 734 431

OFFICES

Australia
Waterman Business Centre
Suite 64, Level 2 UL40
1341 Dandenong Road,
Chadstone, VIC 3148
Australia
Tel: +61 3 8564 8122

United States
6 West 18th Street 4B
New York, NY 10011
United States
Tel: +1 212 645 1111

Shanghai
6F, Building C, 838 Guangji Road
Hongkou District, Shanghai 200434
China
Tel: +86 021 31260822

books@imagespublishing.com
www.imagespublishing.com

The Images Publishing Group Reference Number: 1621

A catalogue record for this book is available from the National Library of Australia

Title: TSK: Selected Works
ISBN: 9781864709216

This title was commissioned in IMAGES' Melbourne office and produced as follows:
Editorial Georgia (Gina) Tsarouhas *Art direction/production* Nicole Boehringer. Thanks to Thais Ometto.

Printed on 157 gsm Chinese OJI matt art paper (FSC®) by Artron Art (Group) Co., Ltd, in China

MIX
Paper from responsible sources
FSC® C019910

IMAGES has included on its website a page for special notices in relation to this and its other publications. Please visit www.imagespublishing.com